THE COMPETENCIES HANDBOOK

Steve Whiddett, BSc (Hons), MSc, C.Psychol., is a chartered occupational psychologist and partner at Pearn Kandola, Oxford. Prior to joining Pearn Kandola in 1991 he was a senior consultant with one of the world's leading test publishers, where he was responsible for development, training and consultancy in job analysis techniques. He has specialised in the areas of job analysis, assessment and development for more than 20 years and for most of that time has been a practising occupational psychologist. He brings a wealth of practical experience to his field, having worked in a range of roles and organisations, including public and private sectors, telecommunications and social services. He currently leads a research programme to identify factors that influence performance at work. This operation will lead to a much wider view of performance and will provide tools for managing performance much more effectively at both individual and organisational levels.

Sarah Hollyforde, MIPD, is a professionally qualified human resources (HR) manager. Her 18 years' experience has been in a number of different roles, including line management and operations management. Although Sarah's background has been primarily in financial services, she has also worked in technology and, more recently, a government agency. She has been involved in a wide range of HR applications, specialising in recruitment, selection, training and development. Her experience in these applications has included the use of a variety of different competency frameworks. Having been involved in the introduction of competency programmes both as an HR manager and a line manager, Sarah brings a pragmatic approach to the subject of competencies.

Other titles in the series:

The Institute of Personnel and Development is the leading publisher of books and reports for personnel and training professionals, students, and for all those concerned with the effective management and development of people at work. For details of all our titles, please contact the Publishing Department:

tel. 020-8263 3387

fax 020-8263 3850

e-mail publish@ipd.co.uk

The catalogue of all IPD titles can be viewed on the IPD website:
http://www.ipd.co.uk/publications

THE
COMPETENCIES
HANDBOOK

Steve Whiddett
and
Sarah Hollyforde

INSTITUTE OF PERSONNEL AND DEVELOPMENT

First published in 1999
Reprinted 2000

Design by Paperweight
Typeset by
Action Publishing Technology Ltd, Gloucester
Printed in Great Britain by
The Cromwell Press, Wiltshire

British Library Cataloguing in Publication Data
A catalogue record for this book is available from the
British Library

ISBN 0-85292-735-5

i)

INSTITUTE OF PERSONNEL
AND DEVELOPMENT

IPD House, Camp Road, London SW19 4UX
Tel: 020 8971 9000   Fax 020 8263 3333
Registered office as above. Registered Charity No. 1038333
A company limited by guarantee. Registered in England No. 2931892

CONTENTS

ACKNOWLEDGEMENTS

We would like to thank all those people who have helped us write this book. In particular we would like to mention Robert Wood, a partner at Pearn Kandola, whose review of our first draft helped us structure the book much as it has ended up. We would also like to thank Anne Cordwent at the IPD who helped us by giving critical but very helpful feedback, and John Curle at the Legal Aid Board who read through our second draft and gave us comments from the line manager's point of view.

There are also many others without whom we would not have been able to complete this book. These include colleagues and clients whose valuable contributions in both our careers have helped shape our views and given us the rich vein of experience from which we drew our examples.

INTRODUCTION

What is in this book?

Competencies are now a feature of many people-management policies and practices. In some organisations competency frameworks are used in one or two applications; in others they form the central focus of all human resource activities.

This book looks at competencies and the applications to which competency frameworks have been put. Chapter 1 investigates different forms of competencies, their origins, and the issues that have to be considered when designing a good competency framework. Chapter 2 takes readers through the key stages of producing a competency framework and introduces three key principles which underpin its development. Each of the subsequent four chapters is devoted to a particular application and discusses the factors that affect that application and how competencies can contribute. The Conclusion to the book draws together the themes raised throughout the book and looks to the future.

A sample competency framework is used to illustrate points made throughout the book. This can be found in Appendix 1 and is referred to throughout the book as the **Appendix Framework**.

In each of the applications chapters we investigate:

❑ the purpose of that application
❑ the factors that influence the application
❑ the contribution that competencies can make.

How should this book be used?

We would advise all readers to read the first two chapters in the order they are presented in the book. The four applications chapters have been written in such a way that they can be read in any order or read selectively depending on the reader's objectives or interests. The Conclusion is a good summary of the key points of the book and emphasises the main themes discussed throughout all the chapters.

Who is the book aimed at?

We have written *The Competencies Handbook* for anyone with an interest in the management of people and/or with an involvement in the introduction or maintenance of a competency framework in their organisation. We have focused most on people who have an understanding of people-management processes but want to know more about competencies. The book is not designed to take someone from complete novice to expert in the space of time it takes for them to read every page. However, we hope that what we have covered in the book will enhance or endorse existing knowledge and highlight areas where readers may feel they need to know more.

1 WHAT DO WE MEAN BY 'COMPETENCIES'?

Organisations have been producing and implementing competencies, or competency-like criteria, for at least 15 years. Recently, a whole industry has developed around competencies and their application, as witnessed in the proliferation of articles, journals, conferences and consultants devoted to the use of competencies.

So what has happened in the development and application of competencies that has generated so much interest? For many organisations the answer is both simple and compelling. Whereas the criteria developed 10 to 15 years ago had been designed for very specific applications – eg one set of criteria for selection and another set of criteria for training needs – competency frameworks promise an opportunity to have one set of criteria which can be applied across the full range of human resource (ie personnel and training) processes.

A common set of criteria for all human resource (HR) processes has two main benefits:

❑ an opportunity to agree a common language for describing effectiveness in an organisation – This common language should help to ensure that individuals in different departments and at different levels in the organisation have a common understanding – for example, of what good leadership looks like or what it means to be effective when working in a team.

❑ an opportunity to achieve a high level of consistency when assessing performance – Whether for selection or in appraisal, all 'assessors' will know what good performance should look like and will know what needs to be assessed and what can be ignored.

In the past it was usually only the specialists – for example, selection specialists and job evaluation experts – who devised and used competency-like criteria. Then it was likely that the criteria were specific solely to their application. Line managers may have encountered competency-like criteria only within the appraisal process.

Recent changes in HR functions and organisational practices have resulted in a much greater involvement of line managers in the full range of what had previously been seen as 'personnel and training activities'. In the past, any discussion with external consultants about the design of an organisation's selection, training or appraisal systems and procedures was usually conducted only with personnel and training specialists. Now it is more usual for consultants to be discussing these activities with a mix of HR specialists and line managers from across the organisation.

The variety of competency users means that there are different views about the definition, applications and structure of competencies and competency frameworks. There is a considerable range of expectations for what can be done with competencies, and large variations in the quality of competency frameworks.

This chapter will cover what is required in order that competencies may be used effectively. To achieve this we need to:

❑ avoid confusion over their definition
❑ structure the competencies in a way which makes them easy to use
❑ understand their role in applications
❑ produce them to standards of appropriate quality.

These areas are tackled below, with examples. A sample competency framework is included at the end of this book (Appendix 1) and will be used as an example throughout. To avoid confusion with other examples used within chapters, we will refer to the sample competency framework as the **Appendix Framework.**

Definitions of competencies

There is a bewildering number of definitions of 'competency'. In part this is because organisations and competency 'experts' seem to prefer their own definitions of competencies to those that have gone before. However, the majority of these definitions are simply variations on two themes which have different origins.

Main themes

The two main themes in the definition of competencies are:

❑ *Descriptions of work tasks or job outputs* – These have their origins in national training schemes, such as the National/ Scottish Vocational Qualifications and the Management Charter Initiative (MCI).

The MCI definition of the concept of competence is 'the ability of a manager to perform to the standards required in employment'. (MCI, 1992)

❑ *Descriptions of behaviour* – These have evolved from the work of researchers and consultants specialising in managerial effectiveness.

Many definitions of behavioural competency are variations on the following definition: a job competency is 'an underlying characteristic of a person which results in effective and/or superior performance in a job' (Klemp, 1980).

Variations typically expand on what the characteristics may be – as, for example, in this much-quoted definition: 'A job competency is an underlying characteristic of a person in that it may be a motive, a trait, a skill, an aspect of one's self-image or social role, or a body of knowledge which he or she uses' (Boyatzis, 1982).

These definitions indicate that a competency is made up of many things (motives, traits, skills, etc) and yet we usually only see evidence of these things in the way somebody behaves. For example, interpersonal *skill* will be demonstrated in how effectively a person negotiates, influences and works in a team. Behavioural competencies describe typical behaviours observed when effective or superior performers apply motives, traits, skills, etc to job-relevant tasks to produce job-relevant outcomes.

Integrating values

In addition to motives, traits and skills, values also influence an individual's behaviour. Many organisations have identified which values they subscribe to and have communicated them to their employees, outlining the part that values should play in the day-to-day management of the organisation. Some of these organisations have integrated values into their competency framework by ensuring that examples of behaviours are consistent with the values.

Flavour of the month?

A public utility issued all staff with a brief statement of the company's values. These values were not integrated into the behavioural statements used in selection or performance management. For example, the values stated that 'customers and suppliers should be treated as partners', whereas behavioural criteria included such statements as 'persist in negotiations to get the best service at lowest cost' and 'establish and maintain charges for maximum profit'. If the organisation's values had been integrated into the behavioural criteria, we would have seen such statements as 'negotiate win–win agreements with best-quality service-providers' and 'provide high-quality cost-effective supplies to customers'. Separating the behaviours and values so evidently meant that individuals did not feel encouraged to behave in a way consistent with the stated values, despite the organisation's best intentions. This gave the impression that values were simply 'flavour of the month', and not that important.

A manufacturing company avoided this situation by identifying behaviours which exemplified the values that had been identified as important for the future of the business. When producing their competency framework, examples of these behaviours were incorporated into the draft competencies. Where behaviours conflicted with the values, these were modified to be consistent with the values. Where examples were missing, these were added. The result was a competency framework which consistently presented examples of the values in action. The values became integral to all people-management processes, and people were encouraged through these processes to behave in a way which was therefore consistent with the organisation's values.

What is the difference between 'competence' and 'competency'?

Many people have wondered if there is any difference between 'competence' and 'competency'. A general convention has developed, although not always followed, which uses 'competence' and 'competency' in the following ways.

❏ An ability based on work tasks or job outputs tends to be referred to as a *'competence'*.

❏ An ability based on behaviour tends to be referred to as a *'competency'*.

In practice, many organisations include tasks, outputs and behaviours in their descriptions of competence/competency, and often blend them together. However, it is far more common for descriptions to be behaviour-based rather than solely task- or job-output-based.

For the purposes of this book we refer to competency(ies) in relation to frameworks based on *behaviours*.

Typical competency framework structures

Organisations present their competencies in different ways. However, most competencies are presented in some form of structured framework similar to the basic framework depicted in Figure 1.

Figure 1
A TYPICAL COMPETENCY FRAMEWORK STRUCTURE

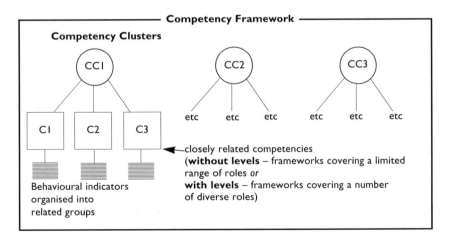

In the structure shown in Figure 1 behavioural indicators are the basic building-blocks of every competency framework. Related behavioural indicators are organised into competencies, either as a straightforward list or within a number of different levels. Related competencies are organised into competency clusters. Each of these is described below, starting with the basic building-blocks – ie the behavioural indicators.

Behavioural indicators

Behavioural indicators are examples of behaviours that would be observed when someone demonstrates competency. In most cases these are examples of effective competency. Examples of poor or ineffective competency, often referred to as contra-indicators, may also be observed and used but they are becoming far less common.

In our **Appendix Framework** the behavioural indicators are examples of effective competency. Behavioural indicators for 'WORKING WITH INFORMATION: Gathering and analysing information' include:

❏ Identifies and uses appropriate sources of information.
❏ Accurately identifies the type and form of information required.
❏ Obtains relevant information and maintains it in appropriate formats.

Competencies

Each competency is a collection of related behavioural indicators. The indicators are organised into one or more lists depending on the scope of the framework.

Competencies without levels

A simple framework – eg one that covers jobs which have very similar behavioural demands – may have a single list of indicators within each competency. In this framework all behavioural indicators would relate to all jobs. For example, a specific framework which covers only senior management jobs in an organisation may include the following behavioural indicators to describe 'Planning and organising':

❑ Produces plans which distinguish between immediate and long-term priorities (eg weeks to three years).

❑ Produces plans which specify clear departmental objectives.

❑ Co-ordinates activities of the department in line with business plans.

A single list is all that is required because all the behavioural indicators will apply to all the senior management jobs.

Competencies with levels

When a framework covers a wide range of jobs with different degrees of demands, the behavioural indicators within each competency may be divided into separate lists or 'levels'. This enables a range within a competency to be described under one competency heading, as is both acceptable and necessary if the competency framework is to meet a wide range of applications and cover a wide range of jobs or roles.

For example, the competency 'Planning and organising' may be relevant to both administrative and management roles. The planning and organising behaviours will be different for these roles – but levelling enables separate lists of planning and organising behaviours to be included in the same framework, avoiding the need for a separate framework for each role.

Using this approach may lead to some competencies' having only one or two levels whereas other competencies may have several levels.

For example, our **Appendix Framework** contains a number of levels for each competency. Most contain three levels, but 'ACHIEVING RESULTS: Planning' contains four, and 'ACHIEVING RESULTS: Deadline management' contains only two.

One method of levelling is to split the behavioural indicators into groups and label them – usually numerically: the more complex the behaviours, the higher the level. Some organisations relate levels directly to job grades. For example, in some frameworks all Level 1 competencies are tied to particular job grades, all Level 2 competencies are tied to the next band of job grades, and so on. But although there is usually some connection between levels and the seniority of a job, it is not always a direct relationship. For example, a senior management position may not require the job-holder to have the highest level of competence for 'managing relationships', whereas a more junior complaints-handling or account-management role may. For this reason, many organisations avoid using existing grade structures to dictate competency levels.

Another method of levelling is by the expected performance of a job-holder. This form of levelling is usually used only where the framework relates to a single job grade or role. For example, a framework may include a list of indicators for

- threshold competency – usually a minimum requirement to perform the job effectively
- outstanding competency – usually an expected level of performance for an experienced job-holder
- negative demonstrations of competency – usually those behaviours which would be counterproductive to effective performance at any level in the job.

The method is intended for when it is necessary to assess different degrees of competency in a group of individuals. For example: when assessing job applicants, the threshold behavioural indicators could be used; when assessing job performance of experienced staff, the outstanding competencies could be used; in both cases the negative indicators may play a part in identifying disqualifying factors or development needs. Generally, by using these levels, degrees of competency can be assessed without adding complexity to the basic competency framework structure.

Competency frameworks that include levels will have one list of behavioural indicators for each level.

Competency titles and descriptions

To help with communication, competencies are usually given a title and some form of description. The competency title is usually very short and distinguishes the competency from other competencies while being descriptive and easy to remember.

Typical examples of competency titles are:

> managing relationships
> teamworking
> influencing
> gathering and analysing information
> decision-making
> personal development
> generating and building on ideas
> planning and organising
> deadline management
> objective-setting.

In addition to the competency title, many frameworks include competency descriptions. There are two main approaches to competency descriptions. The first approach is to produce a summary of the behaviours contained within the competency. For example, a competency such as 'Planning and organising' may be summarised as:

> Achieves results through detailed planning and organisation of people and resources to meet goals, targets or objectives within agreed time-scales.

Where competencies summarise a single list of behaviours this approach works very well.

The second approach is to provide a rationale for the competency in place of a summary – ie a description of why the competency is important to the organisation. This is best used where competency frameworks contain levels of behaviours, because in these cases it is difficult to produce a summary that would cover all roles in the organisation and all behaviours within the competency.

For example, a competency such as 'Influencing' may have five levels. At one level, influencing is largely about presenting clear arguments and facts in support of a case or demonstrating focus and commitment to a product. At another level, influencing includes developing and communicating a vision for the organisation as well as influencing the marketplace and professional bodies. Instead of trying to summarise such a wide range of behaviours, an organisation may produce the following:

> Gaining commitment from others to an idea or course of action through effective influencing is essential for learning, creating

new knowledge, innovation, better decision-making and for developing trust.

In many ways this statement is more useful than the competency summary as it indicates why the organisation values the competency as well as giving a flavour of what the competency covers.

Competency clusters

A competency cluster is a collection of closely related competencies, usually three to five per cluster. Most competency frameworks have clusters of competencies relating to

- thinking – eg analysing and deciding
- acting – eg achieving results
- interacting – eg working with people.

All phrases used within competency frameworks should try to capture the language which is typical within the organisation. In the **Appendix Framework** referred to throughout this book the clusters are entitled

- WORKING WITH PEOPLE
- WORKING WITH INFORMATION
- DEVELOPING THE BUSINESS
- ACHIEVING RESULTS.

Competency clusters are usually given headings like those above to help communicate the scope of the competency framework.

Some organisations also provide cluster descriptions to indicate the nature of the competencies contained within each cluster. For example, 'Working with information' (the title for a cluster) may be described thus:

Working with information includes all forms of information and analysis necessary to produce effective decisions required for day-to-day and long-term efficiency in the business.

Competency framework

'Competency framework' is the term given to the complete collection of clusters, competencies (with or without levels) and behavioural indicators. Frameworks might contain very detailed behavioural indicators for a specific department for a specific purpose or they might contain very broad generic behavioural indicators designed for use across a whole organisation or business unit for a wide range of purposes. The actual degree of detail contained within a competency framework depends on its intended application.

The numbers of competencies within frameworks have reduced in recent years. Whereas it was once common to find frameworks that contained 30 or more competencies, it is now more usual for frameworks to contain no more than 20 competencies, sometimes as few as eight. Many users find between eight and 12 competencies to be the most useful range for a framework.

Larger frameworks often came about because organisations tried to capture all the information required for all applications and all roles, including details about job tasks and outputs and behaviours. Experience has now shown that it is more effective to produce a generic framework, such as our **Appendix Framework**, with guidelines on how to use it for a wide range of applications.

The more competencies that a framework contains, the more difficult it can be to implement. For example, assessors find it difficult to distinguish between competencies in large frameworks because the differences between so many competencies can be very small.

Confusing assessors

A major financial institution had a framework which included separate competencies of 'Negotiating' and 'Influencing'. During assessment centres assessors frequently struggled to assign examples of performance – such as achieving goals in a team meeting – to these competencies. Was this an example of good negotiating or good influencing?

In addition, documentation can become very lengthy and off-putting to users. The thickness of a document is usually inversely related to the number of people who read it – ie the more pages, the fewer the readers.

Size can be important

A few years ago, a government agency developed a very sophisticated competency framework. The framework contained over 60 competencies, each with five levels of complexity. The framework also combined behaviours with tasks and job outputs. This meant that each competency was accompanied by up to seven examples of the contexts in which particular competency levels were considered relevant. Users were finding it almost impossible to apply the framework, and the 200-page reference document undermined any confidence they might have had that they could make the framework work.

The agency thereupon took their competency framework and identified within it the behaviours common to all roles in the organisation. This data was then used to produce a secondary competency framework which contained 12 competencies. Even with levelling for each competency the document was only 12 pages in length. Users found the new framework met their needs, and plans to reintroduce the original framework at a later date were never implemented.

Where *all* competencies in a framework relate to *all* jobs in an organisation or department, the framework is often referred to as a 'core competency framework'. This type of framework does not include competencies which distinguish between jobs within the job groups for which the framework was designed. Core competency frameworks are made up of the competencies which cover behaviours common to all jobs or particular groups of jobs in an organisation. The behavioural indicators in a 'core competency' are therefore generic and, as mentioned earlier, further work needs to be done to make them specific to particular jobs or applications. For example, the **Appendix Framework** has a competency called 'Decision-making' (in the cluster WORKING WITH INFORMATION). The behaviours in Level 1 are:

❑ Follows pre-set procedures where required.
❑ Obtains and uses necessary information to make decisions.
❑ Regularly reviews and agrees scope of decision-making for their role.
❑ Refers decision to others when appropriate.

These are generic statements. If, however, a job-holder's performance was being reviewed in a specific job, then job-specific examples of the behaviours may be used. For a customer services job these could be

- Follows customer service procedures as required.
- Obtains and uses information from customer service database, customer service procedure manuals and makes reference to others to take decisions.
- Does not make decisions outside pre-set authority levels.

Example framework

This structure, with competency clusters as the highest elements and behavioural indicators as the most detailed elements, sets out one of the most common layouts for a competency framework. The **Appendix Framework** is structured in this way. Figure 2 illustrates this using examples from the WORKING WITH PEOPLE cluster.

Applications of competencies

The journal *Competency* regularly reviews applications of competencies, and a few years ago reported the following reasons why organisations had introduced competencies:

performance	clarity of role
cultural change	integrating HR strategy
training and development	enforcing standards/quality
recruitment and selection	reward
business objectives/	motivating employees
competitiveness	increased efficiency
career-succession-planning	Investors In People
skills analysis	equal opportunities
flexibility	

Source: *Competency (1996)*

A very similar list was also produced in the same journal the year before. Contributors to these surveys were provided with open-ended questions seeking up to five reasons for introducing competencies in their organisations. In other words, these

Figure 2
TYPICAL CONTENT OF A COMPETENCY FRAMEWORK

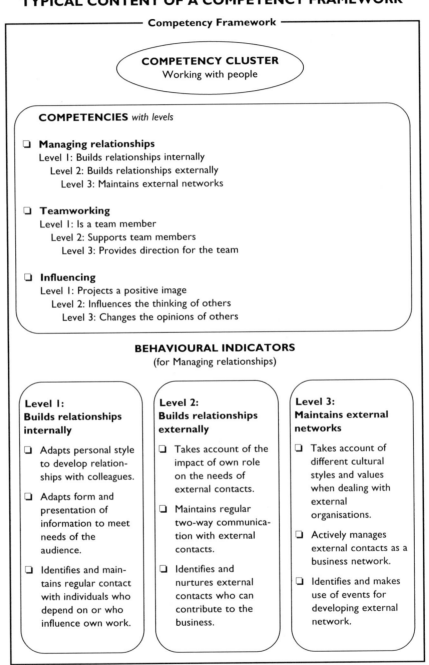

reasons were generated by the users and not predetermined by the journal.

In practice, however, most reasons for using competencies can be captured in these three primary applications:

❑ recruitment and selection
❑ training and development
❑ reward.

The *Competency* journal used these three headings to summarise their more recent surveys.

Although there are many stated reasons for an organisation to introduce competencies (referred to in the early list), many of them will be achieved via the three primary applications.

It may seem surprising that appraisal was not referred to in the summary. Development and reward may be reported separately in terms of the use of competencies because they represent distinct HR functions. Appraisal, or performance management, however, is a process which links these functions.

In addition to a more realistic and practical set of expectations for using competencies, the simplified list of applications

---

A cure for inconsistency

A pharmaceutical company recently merged a number of different business units. Each business unit had its own competency framework and some of the larger units had more than one. Many of these frameworks had been designed for specific applications. This caused confusion as individuals encountered different criteria for appraisal, succession, selection, and so on as they changed roles across the newly integrated business.

The company decided to develop a core competency framework to provide a single set of criteria common to recruitment, training and development, pay and grading, and performance management. This now means that individuals are selected, appraised, developed and rewarded on the same criteria no matter where they are in the company. This has resulted in a much greater level of consistency across people-management processes in the whole company, which individuals are able to recognise for themselves. In addition, specialists in the various HR functions now refer to performance using the same language.

may also reflect the streamlining of HR activities in organisations over the last few years. For example, many organisations now have fewer competency frameworks and these tend to cover a wider range of job roles. In fact, many organisations have been using competency frameworks to integrate their main HR functions and HR activities.

It is now relatively common to find organisations which employ a single competency framework to cover all staff. This framework provides the basic criteria for all activities relating to managing people – ie the primary applications of recruitment, training, development and reward. For example, the **Appendix Framework** is based on a framework made up of competencies and levels which can be applied to all jobs in a marketing company containing about 20 different jobs and nearly 400 staff.

The impact on culture

Although the focus may have shifted to these more mainstream activities, it is worth remembering some of the other applications listed in the *Competency* journal's earlier surveys. Through continuous exposure to competency-based people-management processes, individuals will receive consistent messages about expected behaviour and performance. So it should be remembered that the use of competencies will influence the culture of an organisation – and in most cases, that is the intention.

If culture change has not been considered, or the behaviours in the competencies are not right, there could be a clash between what the organisation needs and the behaviours that people are being encouraged to adopt.

In the example 'Culture clash', the competency framework reflected what some people had thought would be a better way of working. The framework was not based on the way the organisation was constructed at the time, nor did it take account of the aggressive deadlines and targets which senior managers had responsibility for setting and achieving. It was also not the result of any senior management vision for change. In that culture change was not among the reasons for introducing competencies, the demands of the business had clearly been overlooked.

> **Culture clash**
>
> A strongly sales-oriented electronic goods company introduced a set of competencies for junior and middle managers. The behaviours in the competencies centred around collaborative ways of working in an open organisation in which views could be expressed, challenged and championed. All the junior and middle managers were assessed against these competencies and development action plans were drafted to address differences. However, any junior or middle manager who attempted to behave in the new, collaborative style was immediately faced with resistance and hostility from senior managers. It was not long before the development plans were either modified 'to reflect reality' or simply disregarded.

If an organisation intends to effect a culture change with the introduction of a competency framework, the change will not succeed unless it is part of a range of initiatives fully supported by the senior management team.

Being clear about purpose and limitations

As mentioned earlier, many organisations have used competencies to try to integrate HR practices. Success in their efforts at integration is linked to the level of understanding of the role that competencies play in these practices – ie how competencies can be applied in recruitment, selection, training, development and reward. Successful organisations have been those that have used competencies as tools within these applications. They have also been clear about the potential limitations of competencies and what they cannot do. These organisations have been able to keep competencies in their rightful place – in the background of the application. It is the application which is important: competencies just help to make the application effective.

Competencies provide a common set of benchmarks or criteria in the form of behavioural indicators. However, all applications require more than one set of criteria to be effective. For example:

❏ Selection will usually take account of a person's experience, past performance, and job-relevant qualifications.

❏ Training takes account of job tasks and what needs to be achieved.

❏ Development takes account of organisational and individual needs.

❏ Reward is based on job worth as well as the need to reward and motivate individual performance.

The introduction of competencies can increase consistency between these applications. However, the introduction of competencies cannot alone guarantee that these applications will be more effective. As with previous forms of competency-like criteria, effective applications rely on effective and appropriate processes, the right tools and skilled people.

The most comprehensive competency framework, no matter how well designed and appropriate, will not make a bad process good, nor will it compensate for poor training, poor techniques or unskilled users. However, where effective and appropriate processes are allied with appropriate tools and skilled users, competencies can help significantly to improve the standards and consistency of people-management processes within an organisation.

Qualities of good competency frameworks

For a competency framework to be effective it must be usable and fit for its purpose. A competency framework should at least conform to the quality standards listed in Table 1.

The quality standards outlined in Table 1 can provide a good basis for evaluating and testing a framework. Where a framework fails on a standard it may be possible to correct the

Table 1

QUALITY STANDARDS FOR COMPETENCY FRAMEWORKS

❏ clear and easy to understand

❏ relevant to all staff who will be affected by the framework

❏ takes account of expected changes

❏ has discrete elements (eg behavioural indicators do not overlap)

❏ fair to all affected by its use

problem – possible, but not always easy or cost-effective. These standards should be considered long before a competency framework has been produced and readied for implementation. A competency framework should be built to these standards: only then can an organisation be assured that the framework is fit for its intended purpose.

These standards can also be used as a checklist to quality-assure a competency framework during its production.

Each of the quality standards for a good competency framework is explored below.

Clear and easy to understand

A clear competency framework should:

- be unambiguous
- use simple language
- have a simple structure
- have a logical structure.

To be clear and easy to understand a competency framework should reflect the language and phrases commonly used within the organisation. The framework should also be structured in a way that is easy to follow. If competency frameworks are unclear, users become frustrated when trying to use them, and as a result can lose interest in them.

Relevant

The language used in the framework has to be relevant to all the people who are going to use it, whether the framework is generic or specific. 'Relevant to all staff' means that job-holders should recognise the behavioural indicators as examples of behaviours necessary for effective performance in their jobs. In addition, everybody who will use, or be affected by, the framework should be able to see the relevance to the application(s).

In generic frameworks, relevance has to be across all roles. In specific frameworks, relevance may be limited to particular roles or applications.

Relevant to all roles – generic frameworks

Maximum use can be made of competency frameworks when they are relevant to all roles in an organisation or department. 'Relevance to all roles' means that the competencies must describe, in generic terms, behaviours which are essential for effective performance in all roles covered by the framework. It is essential that behavioural indicators have direct relevance to job demands and that they are examples of behaviour demonstrated when those job demands are fulfilled effectively.

Relevant to the application or role – specific frameworks

Where competencies are being developed for a specific application or role, the competency framework should be relevant to that application or role. For example, a competency framework produced specifically for selection must have a sufficient number of detailed behavioural indicators to allow assessors to recognise competency during the assessment process.

Takes account of expected changes

If a competency framework is to stay relevant, it must take account of expected changes which are likely to affect the way in which the organisation operates. These changes are incorporated into competency frameworks by including behaviours which describe the way individuals will need to go about their jobs in the short- to medium-term future.

Competency frameworks should also take account of the vision of the future which the leaders of the organisation are using in setting targets and plans. To stay relevant, a competency framework must take account of

- changes in the organisation's environment
- the introduction of new technology
- visions of the future which leaders are using to inform their decisions.

Discrete elements

One of the main uses for competencies is as criteria in assessment. This may be assessment for selection or assessment for performance appraisal or assessment for succession. The structure of a competency framework will have a major influence on the ease and accuracy of assessments. It is therefore important that each of the competencies has discrete elements. Without them it will be difficult for assessors to know to which competency they should assign an example of effective performance. A few simple rules, such as those below, can be used to avoid confusion in the application of competencies:

- One competency must not depend on another competency.
- Competencies and indicators must appear in only one place in the framework.
- Competencies must not relate to more than one cluster.
- Indicators must not relate to more than one competency.
- Indicators must not relate to more than one competency level.

Behavioural indicators are the working part of the competency when used in assessments. To help to ensure that the behavioural indicators are capable of doing their job, they should

- describe directly measurable (ie observable) examples of an individual's competency

  – *eg keeps colleagues informed of changes to work priorities; produces detailed plans for achieving objectives*

- describe just one piece of behaviour or evidence – it should not be possible for an individual to be good at one part of the indicator and poor at another

- not be duplicated across competencies or levels – it should not be possible for an example of an indicator in one competency or competency level also to be an example of an indicator in another competency or competency level

- include a verb clause: indicators describe what a person does

  – eg *keeps colleagues informed* of changes to work priorities; *produces detailed plans* for achieving objectives

- include enough contextual information to make the action meaningful – ie indicate why the person is performing the action

  – eg keeps colleagues informed *of changes to work priorities;* produces detailed plans *for achieving objectives.*

Fair to all

If each of the above quality standards are met, then a competency framework should be fair to all who will be affected by it. However, a framework could meet the above quality standards but still institutionalise, and inadvertently encourage, unfair biases in organisations. This can occur when insufficient attention has been paid to potential sources of bias – for example, a management competency framework compiled using data collected only from older, white, male managers. Although meeting all the other quality standards, the framework may not be fair to everyone because it may exclude behaviours observed in effective managers who do not come from this sample.

In brief

Competencies can be defined in many ways, but most competency frameworks are now based on behavioural statements. Clarity within the actual definition for a competency framework in a specific situation is essential. This clarity can be achieved by identifying the purpose or purposes for which the competency framework is to be used.

For ease of use, competency frameworks should be kept simple. Organisations have found it much easier to implement generic frameworks with clear user guidelines rather than to try to make frameworks cover the demands of all applications for all roles.

Competencies provide a common set of criteria which can be applied to a range of people-management activities. To be effective, these activities will also require

- additional information
- clear processes
- skilled users.

Competencies can enhance the effectiveness of people-management activities in an organisation but they cannot, in themselves, guarantee it.

The quality of a competency framework will influence its ease of use and its longevity. A well-designed competency framework will:

❑ have a clear structure
❑ use words and phrases normally found in the organisation.

Whatever the purpose of a competency framework it should relate to all

❑ current and future staff who will be affected by it
❑ current and known future organisational needs.

Attending to these points should result in, but does not guarantee, a framework that is fair to all who will be affected by it. Potential sources of unfair bias can be subtle. Quality standards must be used in the production of a competency framework to ensure

❑ fairness
❑ relevance
❑ clarity
❑ discreteness
❑ longevity.

References

BOYATZIS R. E. (1982) *The Competent Manager: A model for effective performance*. Chichester, John Wiley & Sons.

Annual survey of competency frameworks. *Competency.* Vol. 4, No. 1, autumn 1996.

KLEMP G. O. Jnr (1980) *The Assessment of Occupational Competence*. Report to the National Institute of Education, Washington, DC.

The Management Charter Initiative (1992) *Introducing Management Standards*, London, MCI.

2 PRODUCING A COMPETENCY FRAMEWORK

Generic competency frameworks (ie those containing generic behaviours as described in the previous chapter) are a move away from the application-specific frameworks of the past. However, the potential advantages of the competency framework bring important new challenges.

A competency framework has two very important characteristics:

- ❑ It must be relevant to all those who may benefit from its use.
- ❑ It must meet the needs of a wide range of possible applications.

These characteristics can be achieved if certain principles are followed throughout the process of producing the competency framework, and if a disciplined process is followed for producing it.

Key principles for producing competencies

Three principles must be followed when producing a competency framework in order to ensure that it meets the quality standards outlined in Chapter 1.

1 Involve the people who will be affected by the framework.
2 Keep people informed about what is happening and why.
3 Behaviours described in the competencies must be

relevant to all those who will be affected by them as well as to organisational needs and intended applications.

Key principle 1 – Involve people

A competency framework is a useful tool for anybody in an organisation who is involved in managing behaviour – in practice, that should be everybody. It is not surprising, therefore, to find that virtually everybody in the organisation will have a view about the competencies their employer has introduced or is planning to introduce. The views held by potential users will influence their enthusiasm for the competencies, so organisations should find out what these views are *before* the competencies have been finalised. Better still, the users should be involved in producing the competencies.

A sensitive situation

A public utility was introducing major changes to supervisory roles. The change process included the identification of competencies for the new supervisor role and the assessment of existing supervisors against these competencies. As a result of the assessments some job-holders would be offered regrading or a move to a non-supervisory role. The situation was very sensitive.

Before the competencies were produced, everybody who would be affected by them was informed about why they were being produced and how they would be used. In addition, representatives from the relevant groups were involved in providing information and in reviewing the competencies as they were being developed. Despite the sensitivities, the competencies were accepted by all who would be affected by them, including union representatives.

What about us?

Recently, an insurance company experienced difficulty getting a new competency framework implemented. Potential users questioned the relevance of the competencies to their business area – when challenged, they criticised the wording and structure of the competencies. To explore this further, potential users were interviewed.

The message from the interviewees was very clear: potential users felt

> that the competencies were being imposed on them. The strong
> criticisms this group made about the competencies were their way of
> demonstrating their objections to this imposition. In this way they
> were obstructing the introduction of the framework.

Why were the competencies acceptable in the first, more sensitive, situation but not acceptable in the second situation? The
first situation involved everybody likely to be affected by the
competencies in the production of those competencies. In the
second situation, competencies had been developed by a small
group within the corporate business which then asked the
operating businesses to introduce them locally. In the first
situation users were involved, whereas the second situation
alienated the users.

Involvement does not require everybody to be involved in
every stage when producing the competency framework.
Involvement can vary from keeping people informed about the
purpose and progress of producing the competency framework,
to getting some of the key users integrated as part of the
production team. Typically, the greatest level of commitment
to a competency framework has been most easily achieved
when all individuals across an organisation have been involved
in at least some aspects of producing the framework.

Key principle 2 – Keep people informed

How to keep people informed, and what to inform people
about, are critical considerations when producing a competency framework. Careful planning is essential to ensure that
people know what to expect.

Everybody who will be affected by the competency framework should, at the very least, know three important pieces of
information:

❑ why it is being produced
❑ how it is going to be produced
❑ how it is intended to be used.

To communicate this, some or all of the following points will
need to be considered:

❑ what will happen – ie key activities such as interviews,

meetings, testing drafts
- why these activities are necessary
- when the key activities will take place
- what is expected of the people in the organisation
- what individuals' roles in the design process will be
- why individuals have been asked to make a particular contribution – eg as an interviewee
- why individuals may not have been asked to make a particular contribution.
- who to contact for further information.

The degree of involvement in the production process will determine how much a person needs to know.

Good communication removes potential obstacles to producing competencies and reduces or eliminates difficulties when the time comes to implement them. For example, producing competencies requires the collection of job information. A great deal of this information will be collected from job-holders. It is easier to gain the co-operation of job-holders when they know why information is being collected and what their role is in providing this information. When people are asked to provide something without knowing why it is needed, individuals tend to produce their own explanations, often assuming the worst. It is hard to collect objective information about a job when job-

---

It can 'end in tears'

Several years ago a consultant went to interview job-holders as part of a project for producing competencies. That week, in another part of the organisation, there had been some redundancy announcements. Unfortunately, the organisation did not inform interviewees about the purpose of the interviews or brief the consultant about the redundancy situation. Interviewees were suspicious about the real purpose of the interviews and started to draw their own conclusions.

The consultant's first interview lasted only a few minutes – the interviewee did not co-operate and ended the interview by throwing paperwork against the wall and walking out.

Fortunately, such extremes of poor communication and such strong reactions are very rare.

holders believe their performance is being assessed or that jobs may change dramatically as a result of the interview.

Key principle 3 – Create competencies that are relevant

To ensure that competencies are relevant across an organisation it is essential that job information is collected about jobs which represent the range of work in the organisation. Failure to adhere to this principle means that commitment to the competencies could be minimal, or non-existent, later on. It is easier for users to see the relevance of competencies for their area when they know their department or function has contributed to the production of the competencies.

The language used in a competency framework will inevitably be fairly broad when the framework relates to a variety of departments or functions and to a range of applications. For example, a behaviour which is to be assessed for a specific job can relate directly to that job – eg 'Deals promptly with insurance claims.' However, this example behaviour is unlikely to be relevant to all jobs in the organisation. A more general behaviour relevant to all jobs might be 'Deals promptly with requests from internal or external customers.'

Behaviours described in competencies must be relevant to all people irrespective of sex, age, or race. For example, many management competency frameworks are based on male perceptions of the manager's role and may also have been developed using all-male teams of jobs analysts. There are many examples where male stereotyping in the descriptions of behaviour make the competencies less relevant to a more diverse population of males and females.

If some behavioural indicators include statements about physical ability, it is important that they are absolutely necessary. Assumptions about physical characteristics required to undertake tasks must be avoided.

Finally, a common criticism of competency frameworks is that they capture a moment in time. If production of a competency framework focuses only on what is important today, the rapid rate of change in not-for-profit, public- and private-sector organisations will quickly make the framework redundant. It is essential that a vision of the future is encompassed when developing a competency framework. In considering relevance,

---

Avoiding unfairness

A water company was developing core competencies for a group of operational roles. In analysing these roles, such phrases as 'physically agile' were generated from interviews. Although this characteristic was relevant to particular aspects of some of the jobs being analysed (eg surveying construction sites), it was certainly not relevant to all jobs. Including the characteristic could have resulted in unfair discrimination when recruiting for jobs that did not require the characteristic. The behaviour was therefore not included in the framework.

The work done on developing the competency framework had identified that physical disability was not a restriction on effective performance in many roles. A positive consequence of this was that the organisation no longer considered physical disabilities a bar to selection for the majority of existing roles.

---

current and expected demands must be balanced with expected changes.

Key steps in producing a competency framework

Investing time and effort in developing a competency framework is essential. In some ways a competency framework is similar to the foundations that underpin a house. Once it is in place, many procedures will be built using the competency framework as their foundation. Get it right, and future activity can focus on ensuring that the competency framework stays relevant and helping users to apply it – ie general housekeeping. Get it wrong, and future activity surrounding the use of the competency framework will be at best helping frustrated users and at worst repairing damage to the organisation – eg papering over cracks and shoring up structural problems.

Through the implementation of people-management procedures the competencies will shape behaviour in the organisation. Getting the competency framework right should not be left to chance. Producing a competency framework is a structured and disciplined task. Within this task, specialist skills are needed and particular analysis techniques are employed.

There are so many analysis techniques and organisational variables that it is not possible to state that any one particular

approach to producing a competency framework is the right
and only way. Despite the range of techniques, it is reassuring
to report that a sequence of general stages can be identified for
producing a competency framework:

- getting buy-in from key people
- clarification of the purpose
- planning the project
- putting a data-gathering/-analysis team together
- choosing analysis techniques
- data-gathering
- preparing data for analysis
- data analysis
- drafting the competency framework
- validation of the draft competencies
- revisions and finalising the competencies
- launching the framework.

Many organisations have successfully produced competency
frameworks using this sequence. But although the organisations may have followed the same stages, within each stage
the tasks and techniques may have been very different – to
meet the particular circumstances and needs of each organisation.

Following this sequence will only take you so far: skill is
required to complete many of the tasks, and certain conditions
are required to carry out the tasks effectively. However, having
a structure at the outset for producing the competency framework will make success easier to achieve.

The remainder of this section expands on the stages listed
above and focuses mainly on the production of a core competency framework. Comments are included to indicate how
producing application-specific competencies might differ from
an approach for producing generic competencies.

Getting buy-in from key people

Key people that need to be 'bought in' to the production of a
competency framework will include budget-holders as well as
potential users of the competencies. Getting buy-in at the

outset of the project is essential. Buy-in includes a commitment for resourcing the production of the competency framework as well as commitment to using the competencies. All three 'Key principles' need to be considered at this stage.

Management buy-in

A major brewing company introduced a competency framework for its executive management roles as part of an initiative to develop closer links and a common identity across the business. The brewery company had grown over the years, acquiring a number of operating sites. As a result, each site tended to have its own way of doing things and its own identity. The HR director worked with other board members to identify a way of unifying the attitudes and behaviours of executive managers across the different sites. A competency framework was considered a key tool to achieve this because it would provide managers with a consistent model of the behaviours necessary within their roles. In this example, buy-in was obtained at the highest level.

Buy-in was also obtained from the executive managers. This was achieved by presenting a clear business case for the need to unify attitudes and behaviours, and by openly demonstrating the commitment which board members were making to the project. One example of this commitment was the inclusion of board members in the competency framework production team. Another example was in the involvement of all board members in communications about the project. Overall, the proposal to produce and use competencies was always talked about in business terms. Although the initiative was inspired from within HR, the project was not seen as being owned by that function. From the outset the project was presented and seen as a business need, driven from all business areas.

The above example demonstrates that obtaining buy-in and clarifying the purpose are very likely to occur together.

Clarification of the purpose

In some cases the purpose may appear very clear before buy-in has been achieved. However, in our experience the intended purpose may change while buy-in is being sought. This is not surprising, because involving others means taking account of their views. Some negotiation might be expected, therefore, between clarification of the purpose and commitment to the production of a competency framework.

The purpose of the competency framework will influence what the competencies look like. For example, competencies designed for recruitment into a narrow range of roles will need to contain detailed examples of the behaviours required for effective performance in those roles. Perhaps even more importantly, the purpose can set limits on how the framework can be used. For example, the detailed behaviours required for competencies designed specifically for selection may make the competencies very difficult to use for job-grading. For selection, the competencies must be relevant to a particular vacancy: this form of competency will therefore be specific to a few roles and will describe what is *similar* about them. Job-grading requires competencies to cover all jobs/roles in the grading scheme and to indicate how they *differ*.

At the outset of a competency design project, potential applications should be discussed and a clear agreement reached regarding the intended purpose of the proposed framework. It is possible to collect specific information for all intended applications in the process of producing a generic competency framework. To do so could significantly increase the time and resources needed for the project, particularly the data-gathering stage. It is worth considering both the need to have all this information (and/or the cost of not having it) and the subsequent increase in time and resources before commencing the project. Often organisations overcome this issue by producing a generic competency framework with guidelines. These guidelines outline how users should gather more detailed information for a specific application when required.

All individuals involved in the competency design project should have a thorough understanding of what the intended purpose is. It is therefore worth investing time to ensure that everybody has a common understanding of the purpose and of what is going to be produced. One way to test the understanding of those involved is to ask them to describe what they think the competency framework might look like when it is completed. On examining why an existing competency framework is not working in a particular application or situation, it is often found that different users had different expectations of what was going to be produced. They also had no reason to suspect that what would be produced would not be what they wanted.

***

Somebody was bound to be disappointed

An insurance company was developing a competency framework. One group with a particular interest in selection was expecting a competency framework based on behavioural indicators. Another group of users was planning to start skill-based training programmes and was expecting a set of task-based competencies. Each group of users knew what they meant by competencies – it was just that each group did not want the type of competencies the other group wanted. In addition, the team who were developing the competency framework had their own view of how the framework would be used – ie its purpose.

The user groups had not made their expectations or needs explicit to the development team. The development team did not communicate its views about purpose to the users. Inevitably, the final framework could not adequately fulfil the purposes for which the user groups had intended to use it.

***

Planning the project

With a clear view of the purpose and with commitment of resources to produce the competency framework, it is time to start planning. Collecting and analysing job information can be quite a lengthy process, so this is a good time to identify milestones for the work ahead. When planning, every stage right through to finalising the competency framework should be considered – including how to identify that the framework is ready for launch, and who has to 'sign off' the project.

It is important that the planning is led by someone who fully understands each stage in the production process. Where possible, the analysis team should be included in the planning stage to increase their involvement, understanding and buy-in to the project.

Effective plans should ensure that

❑ the project progresses smoothly

❑ potential obstacles are identified and the effects minimised or eliminated

❑ communication is structured and focused on progress and achievement

❑ possible delays are identified at an early stage.

The planning stage provides an excellent opportunity to ensure that all three 'Key principles' described earlier are incorporated into every stage of the project.

Here is a guide to how each of the 'Key principles' might be applied:

❑ *Involve the people who will be affected by the framework* – Identify everybody who will be affected by the competency framework and consider how, and when, they need to be involved in the project. Ensure that the right people are available at the right times. Build in flexibility for when people are no longer available and for rearranging interviews, etc.

❑ *Keep people informed about what is happening and why* – Consider what needs to be communicated; who needs to be communicated to; when to communicate; what the best medium is for communication. As with the first 'Key principle', apply these considerations to each stage – and don't forget lead times for the production and distribution of material.

❑ *Behaviours described in the competencies must be relevant* – Pay regular attention to the intended purpose of the competency framework. At each stage in the project ensure that relevant techniques are used and that appropriate information is collected for compiling the competency framework.

In addition, although not essential at the planning stage, it is worth considering how the framework will be managed and kept up to date after it has been launched. There are three reasons for considering this when planning:

❑ The process for ongoing monitoring of the framework may indicate who to involve in the various stages of the production project. For example, in a large organisation each department may have a representative in charge of identifying changes required in the framework. These individuals could be identified and included in the project at an early stage. This way they would have a thorough understanding of the framework and its purposes.

❑ How the framework will be kept up to date, and who by, should be considered – especially if the framework covers the whole organisation. Issues such as the production and distribution of updates should also be considered. Without one point of control, the newly-launched framework is in danger of evolving into many 'tailored' versions as each part of the organisation updates it with changes.

❑ Explaining that there will be a system for updating the framework, and outlining how people may input to that process, will help buy-in when the framework is launched. All staff should know that the final framework is not 'set in stone' for ever.

The updating process must be communicated carefully. The process should not be seen as an excuse for launching a poor framework, nor should it suggest that the framework is never quite finished.

Putting the data-gathering/-analysis team together

One of the questions posed earlier for planning the data-gathering was 'Who should collect the data?' For maximum ownership, a range of individuals from within the organisation should undertake this task. Optimally, the team should be made up largely – ideally completely – of organisational staff. Where there is an insufficient number of organisational staff available, or where there is a lack of skilled people available, organisations frequently rely on external experts.

A very effective compromise in the make-up of the data-gathering team is to combine internal staff with external experts. There can be particular advantages to using external experts in some parts of the data-gathering. Work required in sensitive areas within the organisation – for example, where major changes are under way – and any work involving senior managers is often delegated to external experts.

Four to eight job analysts, depending on the diversity of roles and the size of the organisation, will make an effective-size team. Teams as large as eight are usually necessary only where large amounts of data need to be collected in a short space of time. If possible, teams should be restricted to a maximum of six analysts.

As in the sample of job-holders, members of the team should, where possible, represent the diversity of people in the organisation by, for example, sex, ethnic grouping and age. However the team is made up, it is essential that everybody in the team is trained and skilled in the use of all the data-gathering techniques to be employed during the project. Data-gatherers involved in using all the data-gathering techniques develop a more rounded view of the organisation and the demands its jobs place on job-holders. This is particularly useful when the team come together with all the data and begin to try to make sense of it at the analysis stage.

It helps the data analysis if team members are able to deal with ambiguity in the use of language and uncertainty regarding the likely outcome of the analysis. Because individuals will be grouping together what they consider to be related behaviours, anyone who has difficulty in identifying alternative interpretations for some statements is likely to find data analysis – which can involve reviewing thousands of statements – a bit too challenging.

Choosing analysis techniques

There is a wide variety of techniques specifically designed for collecting information about jobs and work. These techniques fall within the area of job analysis. Every technique has its pros and cons:

❑ No single technique is sufficient for all data collection.
❑ Not all techniques for analysing jobs suit all situations.

For example, observation techniques work very well for jobs which contain manual activities but they are not well suited to analysing mental activity such as thinking or reasoning. In addition, the structure or politics within an organisation might dictate a particular approach. For example, it is sometimes necessary to interview certain people only because leaving them out could undermine future use of the competencies. In this situation it is better to provide a structure for the individuals' contribution than to leave them to make unstructured criticisms.

It is common practice when producing a competency framework for three or four different job-analysis techniques to be used in combination. For example, when collecting information about the future direction of an organisation it is usually most effective to do it in a group session with members of the board and senior managers. When collecting information about important activities within a specific job, a structured technique for interviewing a job-holder is more effective. To identify where jobs are similar or different, a group session with a range of job-holders may be the most effective technique.

Although some techniques are easy to learn and easy to use, *all* techniques require training and practice before they can be used effectively.

Data gathering

The main objectives for this stage are:

❑ to collect examples of behaviours relevant to effective performance in the organisation
❑ to identify behaviours which may be necessary for effective performance in the future.

It is important that all relevant information is gathered. Some information can be taken from existing documents; other information must be collected from individuals. Sources of data include:

❑ business plans
❑ strategy documents
❑ statements of organisational principles and/or values
❑ examples of what job-holders do
❑ examples of what job-holders produce
❑ job-holders' views about their own jobs
❑ managers' views about the work of job-holders
❑ training documentation
❑ job descriptions

❑ regulatory information

❑ customers' and suppliers' views about the organisation

❑ customers' and suppliers' views about the employees of the organisation

❑ specialists with knowledge of the job as it is – eg trainers

❑ specialists who have knowledge of how jobs will change – eg IT experts.

The type of data to collect will be influenced by the intended purpose of the competency framework. For a generic competency framework, broad descriptions of behaviour taken from a wide range of examples of effective performance are needed. A framework which is to be used for a particular application needs to contain data more specific to the intended application. In both cases, information about the direction of the business and a wide range of examples of effective behaviours needs to be collected.

Table 2 describes the level of data-gathering required when producing a competency framework.

This stage provides an excellent opportunity for involving people. Involvement may be through:

❑ their providing information about their job

❑ their providing views about the work of others

❑ their identifying changes and how they will affect the way people go about their work.

Not all job-holders need to be included in this stage. There will be an opportunity to involve more of them in the later stage of 'validating the draft framework'.

To ensure that the competency framework will be relevant right across an organisation it is important to collect information about jobs right across the organisation. For example, to create a generic competency framework a sample of jobs should be analysed from each department or function and a sample of jobs should be analysed across all roles (eg administration, operations, technical, management). One form of sampling is to take a series of diagonal slices through the organisation, as in Table 3.

For each shaded box two things would usually take place:

Table 2
THE LEVEL OF DATA-GATHERING REQUIRED WHEN DESCRIBING BEHAVIOURAL INDICATORS

		APPLICATION	
		Specific	**General**
J O B	**Specific**	*eg recruitment for all team leaders* Gather data: ❏ specific to the application ❏ within the identified jobs/roles ❏ from the relevant business unit(s).	*eg all applications, for all team leaders* Gather data: ❏ relevant to all applications ❏ within the identified jobs/roles ❏ from the relevant business unit(s).
R O L E	**Generic**	*eg recruitment for all jobs* Gather data: ❏ specific to the application ❏ across all jobs/roles ❏ across the whole organisation.	*eg all applications, for all jobs* Gather data: ❏ relevant to all applications ❏ across all jobs/roles ❏ across the whole organisation.

Table 3
EXAMPLE OF SAMPLING METHODOLOGY FOR DATA-GATHERING IN A LARGE ORGANISATION

Roles \ Functions	Marketing	Sales	Production	Distribution	Packaging	Personnel	Finance
Senior managers	■		■		■		■
Middle managers		■		■		■	
Junior managers	■		■		■		
Team leaders		■		■		■	
Administrative staff	■		■		■		
Operational staff		■		■		■	

❑ a selection of job-holders would be interviewed about their own jobs

❑ a selection of line managers would be asked to identify behaviours which differentiate good performance from less good performance among their direct reports.

In addition:

❑ A sample of job-holders from each horizontal slice of the organisation (ie with similar roles in different functions) could be brought together in group sessions. These groups might identify similarities and differences between jobs within similar levels across the organisation.

❑ Changes likely to affect how people go about their work could be explored using interviews and/or workshops. These sessions would be likely to include senior managers and other individuals with knowledge of imminent changes.

The sample of job-holders who contribute to the data-gathering should represent the diversity of people in the organisation by, for example, age, sex or ethnic group.

The actual number of job-holders that might be involved during this data-gathering stage would depend on how different or similar roles are across the organisation. The more differences there are between roles, the greater the number of people needed in the sample. So, for instance, organisations with a wide range of technical specialists might need to include a large sample of job-holders. Where roles are very similar across the organisation, fewer people need to be included at this stage. Although a department store may employ many staff, for example, only a few people from each key job (sales assistant, stock-room controller, supervisor, department manager and store manager, perhaps) need to be included. In the latter case, however, involvement of the remaining staff across all stages of the project should be considered.

A large amount of data will be collected by the analysis team. This could range from a few hundred to one or two thousand examples of effective behaviour. Other reference material such as values, and vision and mission statements may also be collected at this stage. The data should also contain views about the behaviours that will be necessary for effective performance following expected changes to working conditions in the organisation. If the data does not have this breadth, the third 'Key principle' regarding relevance has not been adhered to.

A final point about data-gathering is a reminder about the importance of the second 'Key principle'. This stage will suffer significantly if people are not kept informed about their involvement in the project.

Preparing data for analysis

The major objective of this stage is to turn all the data gathered into a draft competency framework. It is also an opportunity to test whether the third 'Key principle' has been adhered to.

First, the data must be 'coded'. A useful approach is to code each behaviour to show where it came from – eg the job, the function, the job analyst and the job-analysis technique.

For example, each statement could be written up in the following format:

Amends deadlines to account for changes to business priorities.	**Analyst:** *Pat Huang* **Job title:** *Supervisor* **Technique:** *Interview* **Function:** *Engineering*

Coding can be set up as a secretarial task to include classification of the behavioural statements. In this way, all the information is being collected in one place ready for use later. Coding and classification have the added advantage that everybody involved in the data analysis will be able to read behavioural statements collected by other members of the data-gathering team and know where, and how, they were collected.

Coding and classification of the statements should be done as the data-gathering progresses so as to avoid delaying the analysis stage.

Data analysis

Most team members seem to enjoy the process of collecting the data. The same cannot always be said of the process for analysing the data. Data analysis, to be effective and to prevent it eroding the enthusiasm of the team, needs to be conducted with sufficient time, preparation and structure. It also helps if all individuals involved in the data collection contribute at this stage.

It is important that the structure of the competencies should be allowed to emerge from the data. A structure should not be 'forced' on to the data in the form of preconceived ideas held by the project team. If this does occur, there is a strong risk that the competencies will simply reflect what the team think or believe should be there.

In the face of so many behavioural statements, starting with a detailed analysis of all the statements will be like trying to wade through treacle. There is a less tiring approach which has proved to be very effective:

1   Ensure that behavioural statements collected during the data-gathering stage have been written up and coded. Separate the statements with their related codings onto individual strips of paper.

2   Divide the team into two smaller teams and provide each team with a full set of the statements.

3   Each team takes some of their statements (a few handfuls – the rest will be used later) and groups related statements into broad categories, aiming to produce a total of no more than four categories. In our **Appendix Framework**, categories produced at this stage were:
    – people
    – analysing
    – achieving
    – business.

4   Each team makes a brief presentation to the other team describing the broad categories they have produced. The teams identify similarities and differences in the categories and decide which three or four categories will be used for the next step.

5   The teams work independently to group *all* of their behavioural statements (including the ones they used in Step 3) into the agreed categories. It is not necessary to dwell long

over the meaning of each statement. The teams will be looking at the statements in more detail later.

6   Taking each category in turn, each team subdivides its statements (still grouped in categories) into smaller groups of related behaviours. This usually produces three or four groups for each category. These are very rough estimates of the final competencies. A number of refinements may occur during this step such that groupings are combined or divided as understanding continues to develop about the behaviours within each of the broad categories.

7   The teams now reconvene and compare their work. The objective is to work together to agree the basic structure of the competency framework – ie the competency clusters and the competencies. This is achieved by:

– taking one broad category at a time

– comparing the groupings of behavioural statements that each team has produced within each category (detailed comparison is not necessary at this stage)

– agreeing to keep groupings as they are, where they match

– exploring the reasons where groupings do not match, and subsequently deciding collectively on a revised grouping.

At this stage the clusters and competencies will not be named because changes may still be made to them.

One outcome of this stage may be that gaps are identified in the gathered data – for example no (or very few) behaviours relating to senior-manager roles. If this occurs, the coding should indicate where additional data must be collected. A few cancelled interviews may perhaps mean a particular group of jobs has not been included. The team should then collect this data before drafting the framework. A well-planned and monitored project usually avoids this problem.

Drafting the competency framework

Data analysis and drafting of the competency framework are usually done as one continuous activity. Even for a fairly modest competency framework, two or three days – with lots of space and no distractions – is usually necessary for these stages. Fortunately, the time does not dramatically increase for larger or more demanding frameworks. It took six people two-and-a-half days to analyse 1500 statements and to draft the competency framework on which the **Appendix Framework** is based.

Following the last step in the data analysis stage, the following steps can be used to produce a draft competency framework:

1   The team produces what it considers to be appropriate titles for individual competencies (referred to as 'groupings' in data analysis). The team then moves on to the competency clusters and develops titles for these (referred to as 'categories' in data analysis). This step may be better done in smaller teams, reconvening from time to time to test their ideas and to reach agreements.

2   Working with just one set of the behavioural statements, the team reviews the statements under each competency title. The team will decide which behavioural statements should be:
   – moved to another competency because they are now more relevant elsewhere
   – discarded because they are considered too vague to be useful
   – simplified because they are too complicated
   – generalised because they are too specific
   – subdivided because they are considered to contain a number of separate behaviours.

   Where statements are rewritten it is important to retain the code(s) from the original statement(s).

3   The team should now eliminate any duplication in the behavioural statements. In this step, all statements which describe the same behaviour are replaced with a single statement. Again, it is important to transfer the codes from the original statements on to the new statement.

4   If levelling is appropriate, the competency levels should be identified directly from the data. A competency framework for which data has been gathered from a number of differ-

ent job roles may require levelling. Two approaches to levelling are:

– *imposing levels onto the indicators by identifying indicators uniquely relevant to existing job grades.*

Where data indicates that jobs genuinely require incremental levels of competencies consistent with increments in job grade, then, fine: the data is there to prove it. This approach is valid as long as existing job-grade structures are to remain unchanged. If job-grade levels are not going to change, then the coding of the data, which took place during data collection, can be used to identify how a competency differs between job grades – eg how 'teamworking' looks for Grade 2 staff and how it looks different for Grade 3 staff.

– *identifying competency levels direct from the data.*

Within the clustered statements there will be clear indications of different contexts in which the behaviours are important. For example, in 'Decision-making' a number of statements may refer to day-to-day decisions. Other statements may refer to strategic decision-making. These are different competency levels. It is obvious that the levels will not apply to all job-holders. Using this approach may result in some competencies' having only one or two levels while other competencies have several levels.

There may be a temptation to produce additional levels (by rewriting behavioural statements) if the analysis team feel that there aren't enough levels in a particular competency. It is inappropriate to try to create levels on this basis.

It is more rigorous and defensible to identify natural levels within the data – eg based on different contexts and levels of complexity.

There is usually an assumption that competency levels are incremental. That is to say that behaviours at one level assume that the behaviours at all previous levels are present. If this is not in fact the case, there needs to be some indication of it in the framework. Competency frameworks which include levels that are not incremental can cause confusion because each relevant level has to be specified in every role profile created from the framework. For example, a senior role may have all levels in all competencies specified. One way of avoiding independent competency levels is to split the competency. For example, if team leadership does not require team membership behaviours, it may be better to split the behaviours into separate competencies rather than keep them all under one 'teamworking' heading.

These steps will result in the production of a first draft of a competency framework. The draft framework can now be checked to ensure it conforms to the quality standards listed in the previous chapter.

At this stage the draft competency framework describes only the current situation and is based on the sample of jobs used during the data-gathering stage.

Validation of the draft competencies

Further testing is necessary to ensure that

❑ the competencies actually relate to all roles in the target population
❑ the draft competency framework is meaningful in the eyes of the intended users
❑ the behaviours actually differentiate between good and less good performance.

This further testing is to assess the validity of the framework.

The term 'validity' is frequently applied in different ways to different things, so it is important to be sure about what the term is intended to mean here. 'Validity' here refers to two things.

❑ Firstly, do individuals who demonstrate the competencies perform their work more effectively than colleagues who do not demonstrate the competencies?
❑ Secondly, do individual job-holders recognise the competencies as relevant and necessary for effective performance in their jobs/roles?

Here is another excellent opportunity to employ the 'Key principles' for producing competencies.

❑ Involve the people who will be affected by the framework – The validation stage provides an opportunity to involve individuals in the production of the competencies who were not closely involved in earlier stages.

❑ Keep people informed about what is happening and why – The validation stage provides an opportunity to communicate how the work of producing the competencies is progressing.

❑ Behaviours described in the competencies must be relevant – The validation stage is a move nearer to ensuring that the competencies can contribute to their intended purpose(s).

Validation of the framework can be undertaken as two distinct tasks. These tasks can be combined.

Task one is to seek structured feedback from a wide range of people in the organisation. This feedback should focus on

❑ the perceived relevance of the competencies for an individual's job

❑ perceptions of job-holders about the language used within the framework.

Matching pairs

A major bank was developing a competency framework. In order to validate the first draft, questionnaires were distributed to 250 pairs of staff in six different departments Each pair of staff consisted of a manager and one of their direct reports. Questionnaires contained lists of behavioural indicators from the competencies on which each direct report rated himself or herself in terms of effectiveness. The managers rated their reports using the same form of questionnaire.

Ratings on performance criteria, such as 'achievement of business objectives', were collected for each direct report. Competency ratings were compared with the performance criteria ratings. The data showed that individuals who scored highly on the performance criteria ratings were consistently rated highly on the majority of the competencies.

This demonstrated that the competencies were a valid way of distinguishing between effective and less effective performers.

This task can be carried out using structured questionnaires or focus groups or a combination of both.

Task two is to test how well the competencies distinguish between effective and less effective performance. To do this it is necessary to collect ratings of job-holders on

❏ the competencies (obtained from both job-holders and their managers)
❏ other performance measures – eg appraisals, productivity.

A statistical comparison is then made between the performance measures and the competency ratings.

At this stage the draft competency framework still relates only to the current situation.

Revisions and finalising the competencies

The competency framework does not yet incorporate all of the data collected in the data-gathering stage. Finalising the framework will be a matter of fine-tuning based on feedback from the validation stage plus the information gathered about

❏ the direction of the business
❏ expected changes which will affect how people go about their work
❏ new organisational principles and/or values
❏ business plans, vision, regulations, etc.

Learning to learn

An FMCG company was introducing new values at the same time as it was finalising a new competency framework. One of the values was about life-long learning. The draft framework did not fully capture, or represent, this value. So, in fine-tuning the framework prior to launch, some indicators were modified where they contradicted the concept of lifelong learning. For a few competencies new indicators were developed to ensure that the value was fully represented in the framework.

When launching the competency framework, the company communicated how its values had been integrated into the framework. As a result, people using the new competency framework understood why they were being encouraged to adopt a new approach to their development.

Launching the framework

Once the framework has been 'signed off', it can be launched within the business. It is important that the first and second 'Key principles' are observed at this time. Communication should be appropriate to the purpose(s) and the population for which the framework was developed. Appropriate communication should reiterate

❑ why the framework was produced
❑ how it was produced
❑ how it is going to be integrated into the various applications
❑ how users will be supported in their use of the framework
❑ how the framework will be kept up to date.

Launching the framework, and making it available, does not guarantee that the framework will be implemented. Implementation requires users to be trained in the use and interpretation of the competencies, and tools may be needed to assist users further.

The process for keeping the framework up to date should be implemented. It is likely that the more specific the framework, the more frequently it will change – particularly in the language used. All people affected by the framework should understand how they can contribute to keeping it up to date. For example, if representatives are appointed to feed the changes through to a central point, people should be made aware who these representatives are and how to raise issues with them.

Developing a specific framework

There are two basic ways to develop a specific competency framework. The first is to produce the framework using the principles and approach described earlier. The second approach is to adapt an existing generic framework to specific situations and applications.

Producing a specific framework from first principles

The steps that need to be undertaken to produce a specific framework are basically those needed to produce the generic framework, but on a smaller scale. The main areas of difference are in:

❏ data collection
❏ data analysis
❏ drafting of the framework.

All previous comments regarding principles and techniques for data collection still apply. The main difference is that data collection can focus much more closely on job- or application-specific examples of behaviours. For example, a specific framework for a narrow range of administration roles could include behavioural statements which refer to specific processes and procedures used in those roles – provided that these statements generalise to other jobs covered by the framework. In addition, the sample of job-holders from which to gather information will be smaller than that for a generic framework. However, it is important to ensure that the sample is large enough to pick up important differences within the jobs for which the framework is being developed. Depending on the number of similar jobs to be covered by the framework, preparing data for analysis – ie coding the data – can usually be simplified where less coding information is needed.

The analysis stage should involve far fewer behavioural statements than the same stage when producing a generic framework. However, the same steps can be applied to the statements. The main difference here is that the more detailed behavioural statements should make sorting of the data easier because it is easier to classify specific behaviours.

When drafting the competency framework, a key consideration should be to ensure that rewording of behavioural statements does not result in the statements' losing their specific focus.

As with the production of a generic framework, the people who produce a specific framework need to be trained and skilled in the use of data-gathering and analysis techniques.

Adapting a generic framework to specific situations and applications

A generic competency framework – ie a framework that applies across the whole business and/or a range of applications – will need tools and procedures to ensure that the framework is usable in specific circumstances. In order to keep the integrity of the original framework the adaptation should adhere to the competencies and structure already in existence. Any major discrepancies should be raised through whatever update procedure is in place.

Generally, there will be two types of users. The first type of user will be the specialist – for example a recruitment specialist – who will need to compile specific examples of competencies to match the job into which he or she is recruiting. The second type of user will, for example, be line managers who require guidance on how to interpret generic behaviours in such situations as performance reviews for specific individuals in specific roles.

For the first type of user, the following applications chapter (page 57) provides some guidance in adapting generic competencies. For the second type of user, organisations will need to develop guidelines and supporting tools – eg checklists – to assist them in their use of a generic competency framework. These tools and guidelines should enable users to adapt the generic behaviours to their specific needs within the standards required for behavioural competencies. In using these tools and guidelines, users of the competency framework will also be buying in to the outcomes of such adaptation because it will be their knowledge of specific circumstances which results in a specific framework.

In brief

Producing a competency framework that meets the needs of a wide range of users requires a structured approach. Involvement and communication are essential for developing co-operation in the production of the framework and for nurturing ownership and commitment to using the framework. Ensuring the relevance of the framework to individual and organisational performance must be another visible goal during the production of the framework.

To achieve these goals a planned analysis of relevant jobs/roles is required which also looks at expected and imminent changes that will affect the way individuals go about their work. The production of a competency framework is a process which combines views of what happens within jobs or roles with visions of the future. The techniques required to gather the necessary data must be applied with discipline and skill to ensure that the data collected is as objective as possible. It is also important that, where possible, all who will be affected by the framework will have contributed to its production at some stage. If the organisation is too large to include all people, then those who are included must be recognised as truly representative by everyone who will be affected by the framework.

The definitions and structure of the competency framework are dictated by the data itself. Imposing pre-set structures or ideas onto the data when there is no evidence to support them undermines the rigour and effort invested in collecting the data.

No matter how thorough the data collection and process for drafting the competency framework, it is essential that the relationship between the competencies and job performance is not assumed or taken for granted. Relevance of the competency framework should be evident to its users in the language used, but it should also be tested and proven before the framework is implemented.

Once the framework is launched, users must be provided with necessary support, training and tools to implement the framework. A process should also be implemented for keeping the framework relevant and up to date.

Further reading

GHORPADE, J.V. (1988) *Job Analysis: A handbook for human resource directors*, New Jersey, Prentice-Hall.

PEARN, M.A. *and* KANDOLA, R.S. (1993) *Job Analysis: A manager's guide*, 2nd edition. London, Institute of Personnel Management.

3 USING COMPETENCIES IN SELECTION

The purpose of selection

We use 'selection' here to refer to all processes in which individuals are assessed for placement into roles within an organisation, whether the applicants are internal or external to the organisation, permanent or temporary. Whatever the reason, the primary purpose of selection is to place individuals who can make effective and worthwhile contributions to an organisation into appropriate jobs or roles.

Recent books and articles have referred to 'competency-based selection'. The term can be misleading, for selection should always include other assessment criteria. Even though competency-based selection may place a greater emphasis on behaviour than other forms of selection, competencies are unlikely to be the only criteria used.

Although competencies are important in selection, they are not sufficient in themselves to ensure an effective selection process. Effective selection requires skilled selectors to assess applicants, using relevant assessment criteria and relevant assessment methods, before taking decisions about the suitability of applicants for a particular vacancy.

Factors to be taken into account in selection

Competencies contain behaviours observed when effective jobholders undertake job-relevant tasks within an organisation. Competencies are therefore best assessed when potential jobholders are observed while undertaking job-relevant tasks in a realistic organisational environment.

Selection is not just about assessing job performance. In the early stages of selection, selectors may need to screen out applicants who are unsuitable before the more costly process of assessing applicants while they undertake realistic job tasks. Criteria such as qualifications and experience may feature more at the early stages of selection whereas competencies may become more prominent criteria later in the process. Nevertheless, competencies can make important contributions at most stages in selection.

The contribution of competencies to selection

Competencies provide a framework for giving and collecting information about jobs and job applicants. Competencies provide

❑ examples of behaviours necessary for effective performance in the job
❑ words that can be used in advertisements
❑ criteria for choosing and designing assessment methods
❑ benchmarks for decision-making
❑ a structure for giving assessment feedback
❑ a set of criteria for monitoring the selection process.

Behaviours necessary for effective performance in the job

Where assessment criteria are written in broad or general terms, as in generic/core competencies, the criteria may be subject to different interpretations from different users. In some applications this can be useful, but in selection it can reduce the potential reliability of assessment and selection decisions. Another feature of the generic competency framework is that it covers all jobs. However, it is unusual for all jobs in an organisation to require job-holders to be equally competent in all competencies in a framework.

There are three things that can be done to improve the contribution competencies make to selection:

1   Identify the competencies or competency levels which are *critical* for effective performance in the job. This will minimise the total number of competencies that could be

assessed in selection. Six to eight critical/essential competencies are usually sufficient.

2   Identify competencies which might be used to decide
between applicants who are equally suitable on the critical
competencies. These are 'desirable competencies', and
although not critical they must be important for performance in the job.

3   Identify detailed examples of the generic behavioural indicators – ie what these generic behaviours actually look like
in the target job.

Identifying recruitment-critical competencies

There is always a trade-off between assessment of every possible factor that will affect performance and the resources (eg
time, money and people) available. Restricting competency
assessments to competencies that are critical for performance
at the required level reduces the time and effort needed to
develop and manage selection without seriously undermining
the process. By limiting the number of competencies, the
recruitment process also counters accusations of 'cloning' – ie
trying to make all job-holders the same. By using only those
competencies that are essential to the job there are still many
ways in which job holders will differ.

Here is one approach including considerations for identifying 'recruitment-critical' competencies for a job or role.

❏ List the most critical job tasks required to meet the job
purpose.

❏ List the competencies that would be required to undertake
each of these tasks.

❏ Rank these competencies in the order of their importance
for completing the tasks. If the framework includes levels,
identify them in the same way.

❏ Consider whether individuals will be able to develop quickly
to an acceptable level in some of the competencies once in
the job. If so, these competencies could be left out of the
selection processes.

❏ The remaining competencies should be the ones that are
essential.

These steps can be undertaken together with existing job-holders and/or their managers because these individuals should have the most realistic view of the job. Involvement also enhances buy-in to the resulting criteria and selection decisions.

A similar approach can be used for new jobs provided that the key tasks and responsibilities have been identified for the new job. In this situation, individuals with knowledge of the demands of the tasks and responsibilities of the new job can be used to identify recruitment-critical competencies. These individuals may have experience of component parts of the new job – that is, they may currently or previously have undertaken or managed some of the tasks or responsibilities. In many cases a group of people who have experience of different component parts of the new job can, between them, provide a comprehensive view of the whole job.

Critical versus desirable competencies

Where an assessment process uses several assessment criteria – eg competencies – it is usually not difficult to choose between applicants. However, it can happen that some applicants appear equally suited for a vacancy. It is useful to be prepared for such occasions by identifying additional competencies which are important in the job. Identifying these 'desirable' competencies also helps to check that 'critical' competencies really are critical.

Make-your-mind-up time

A major financial institution was running a number of assessment centres to recruit in to a team leader role. During the job analysis stage, 'influencing' was deemed to be critical. It was agreed that if a candidate achieved an unacceptable score on any critical competency the candidate would be rejected.

One candidate on the assessment centre was rated high or acceptable on all competencies except 'influencing', in which his score was 'unacceptable'. The managers conducting the assessments agreed that the candidate had demonstrated that he could do the job despite being rated unacceptable on influencing. The managers decided to override the original rules of the assessment centre, saying that influencing was important but not critical for performance in the job.

In the above example, a competency previously thought critical actually was not. A challenge for all critical criteria at this stage in the process is:

> *If an applicant achieved an unacceptable score on this selection criterion but highly on every other one, would we still wish to progress his or her application?*

If the answer is 'yes', then that criterion is not a critical one.

Competencies identified as important but not critical can be included in the later stages of selection to help where there are too many candidates who make the grade on critical competencies.

Refining competencies

Once the 'recruitment-critical' competencies/levels have been identified, detailed examples of the behavioural indicators can be developed.

The broad behavioural statements – ie the behavioural indicators – within generic frameworks must be made more precise when used in selection in order to increase the consistency of assessments. Behavioural indicators are needed which provide clear and detailed examples of what each competency looks like when observed in the particular vacant job or role. Ideal people to supply this detail are job experts such as existing job-holders and their managers. For each generic behavioural indicator these experts need to answer the question, What would this look like in this job?

Detailed indicators can be developed using

- ❏ an interview
- ❏ a facilitated group approach
- ❏ questionnaires.

It is important that each detailed indicator is both relevant to the competency level and the job, and that it conforms to the standards for indicators described in Chapter 1.

Although behaviours need to be job-specific, they must not be so specific that they could be demonstrated only by someone who is already doing the job. Behaviours must be worded in a way which ensures that they will not exclude individuals who have demonstrated similar behaviours in other situations. For example, although 'Checks sales figures for electric toasters with inventory' is an example of 'Establishes accuracy of information', it is too specific for use in selection. Using this specific example excludes anyone who hasn't worked in sales or with electric toasters.

Where assessment exercises are being designed for specific vacancies, behaviours can be made specific to both the vacancy and the outputs sought in the assessment method(s). Furthermore, different situations within the job may require different information to be used in different ways to produce different outputs. For example, in the competency 'WORKING WITH INFORMATION: Gathering and analysing information, Level 2' the type of information the individual is required to work with and the types of output required using the information are not specified.

The generic indicators for 'WORKING WITH INFORMATION: Gathering and analysing information, Level 2' are:

❑ Establishes accuracy and relevance of information.
❑ Extracts key patterns and trends from information.
❑ Identifies links between different sets of information.
❑ Simplifies information for interpretation and presentation.

For a particular assessment exercise, such as a case-study, these indicators may be made more specific to the particular job and assessors may be asked to look for examples of the following:

❑ Highlights inconsistencies in the data relating to production and transportation costs.
❑ Identifies the need to collect further information on new equipment costs.
❑ Discards estimates of staff cover as irrelevant to the key issues.
❑ Uses figures provided in several documents to forecast product demand for the next quarter.
❑ Makes links across materials provided to identify the five key issues.
❑ Presents performance information, to support presentation, in easy-to-interpret charts or graphs.

To ease the load placed on assessors, each assessment method undertaken by applicants should have an accompanying list of role/exercise-specific behavioural indicators to which the assessors can refer when classifying evidence against the competencies.

Using competencies to word job advertisements

Advertisements should aim to attract better-suited applicants while dissuading unsuitable applicants. Sufficient information must be included to minimise different interpretations of what an organisation is looking for.

More and more job advertisements now include competency information as a way of indicating the type of person the organisation is keen to attract. It is not always easy, however, to decide how much competency information should be included at this stage. Just as generic behavioural indicators can lead to inconsistency in assessment decisions, general competency information in advertisements can lead to inconsistency in the suitability of applicants. If only competency titles are used, potential applicants can make up their own minds about what an organisation is looking for.

Informing applicants about the job

Organisations need to communicate the details of vacancies to relevant audiences. The communication – most likely to be an advertisement of some description – has to contain enough information to attract the right applicants.

Compare these two approaches:

Example 1

This role requires people with a proven track record of: Working with people; Working with information; Developing the business; Achieving results.

Example 2

Successful Customer Services staff operate as part of a team, providing support to each other and sharing experiences. The role is demanding and it is important that you are able to adapt your style to the different styles of others and to present information in different ways when customers don't understand you the first time. Written and spoken information feature a lot in the work and it is important that you can quickly spot the information that is important and where to find it.

The first example actually says very little. Many jobs could be described using these competencies, and many applicants could therefore decide they have the necessary experience to make it worth their while applying for the job.

The second example restricts the range of competency information to those competencies which are most critical while providing examples of why the competencies are important. These examples are taken from the behavioural indicators and demonstrate the importance of using everyday language in competencies. Applicants who read the advertisement in Example 2 will have a better idea about whether their experiences match the requirements described.

The wording in Example 2 is much more likely to help applicants to decide whether or not to apply, and therefore increases the proportion of relevant applicants for a vacancy.

Using competencies to choose and design assessment methods

General points

Not all assessments assess competencies

Selection is not just about assessing potential job performance. Other factors may restrict individuals from being employed for specific jobs – for example:

❑ legal requirements to hold a particular qualification: eg Heavy Goods Vehicle (HGV) licence-holder for a driver of HGVs

❑ minimum legal working age

❑ ability to spend time away from home – eg long-haul pilot.

A good selection process will screen out individuals who do not pass basic requirements before assessing potential performance.

Finding the right assessment methods

It is not difficult to find assessment methods for measuring competencies. Most selection processes include several assessment methods, from application forms to simulations of job tasks. The challenge is to find and use the right methods for the specific vacancy.

Assessment methods should be relevant to the vacancy and they should provide consistent measurements. Assessment methods should be tested for relevance and reliability before they are used in a selection process.

Competencies alone are poor criteria for choosing and/or designing assessment exercises. To illustrate this we have compared types of assessment with the processes used when buying a car. While we are not suggesting that people are like cars, we are saying that *processes* undertaken when buying a car (or, indeed, making any major purchase) have similarities to *methods* used when selecting people.

Buying a car

Once a buyer has decided what to look for in a car, he or she must decide how to assess specific cars to identify the one best suited to his or her needs. There is a number of assessments the car buyer can make to help with the selection decision:

- ❏ Look at its general appearance.
- ❏ Use a checklist of essential characteristics.
- ❏ Ask how good the owner thinks the car is.
- ❏ Question previous owners on the history of the car.
- ❏ Look at the handbook and service history.
- ❏ Ask for specific examples of the car's performance.
- ❏ Take it for a test-drive.
- ❏ Make predictions based on technical characteristics of the car.

The car buyer may undertake more than one of the above assessments before making a decision on whether to purchase the car or not. Some assessments will not provide the best measure of a car's suitability. For example, buying a car because it looks OK and the owner says it is a great car to drive is at best going to leave the car buyer unprepared for what is wrong with the car, and at worst leave him or her having made a very expensive mistake.

Short of taking the car away for a few months to try it out, a test-drive is probably the most accurate means of assessing of its suitability. It enables the car to be driven in realistic situations while undertaking tasks that represent the everyday operations the car will be required to perform. For example, if the car is to be used for long motorway journeys with a full load as well as for trips around town, then these conditions should be part of the test-drive.

There are some assessments that a buyer may wish to make before he or she undertakes a test-drive. These assessments will prevent the buyer from viewing a car which does not meet certain basic require-ments. For example, he or she may wish to check that the car has a certain number of seats because, however suitable the car is in other ways, without the right minimum number of seats there would be no point in viewing it.

There are also some assessments the car buyer may wish to make after taking it for a test-drive. These will relate to areas that won't be covered by driving the car. For example, the car buyer may wish to check the car's history by looking at the service book.

The car buyer illustration shows that a thorough process for selecting one car from many contenders requires the buyer to collect a range of different information using different methods of assessment.

Similarly, a thorough process for selecting a few candidates from many contenders requires the selector to compile a range of different information using different methods of assess-ment. As in the car illustration, not all assessment methods are necessarily good ones. There are many different methods used by recruiters – for example:

❏ Assess general 'fit' with the team (first impressions, 'gut feel').
❏ Refer to a checklist of essentials (screening criteria).
❏ Ask how good the candidate thinks he or she is (unstruc-tured interviewing).
❏ Question previous employers on the history of the candi-date (take-up references).
❏ Look at the personal/career history of the candidate (the curriculum vitae, CV).

❑ Ask for specific examples of the candidate's past performance (structured interviewing).

❑ Ask the candidate to undertake tasks similar to those he or she would undertake in the job (work samples and simulations).

❑ Make predictions based on the results of specific tests (psychometric tests).

There are some assessments a recruiter may need to make before passing applicants on to the next stage of a selection process. These assessments prevent wasting time when essential selection requirements aren't met. For example, they may wish to check that applicants have necessary qualifications because, however suitable applicants are in other ways, there would be no point in proceeding with applicants who were not suitably qualified.

An organisation may undertake one or many assessments before making a decision on whether or not they should recruit a candidate. Some assessments do not provide good measures of a candidate's suitability. For example, recruiting someone because they looked as if they would fit in and they gave the right answers when the recruiter had a chat with them would at best leave the employer unprepared for what the new recruit's training and development needs were, and at worst leave them having made a very expensive mistake.

Each type of assessment uses or seeks information in addition to that which can be provided using competencies. See, for example, Table 4.

Table 4
ADDITIONAL INFORMATION REQUIRED BY FORMS OF ASSESSMENT

Type of assessment	Additional information
References	previous history, perceptions of others
Screening criteria/CV	previous experience, qualifications, personal circumstances
Interview	previous experience, knowledge, attitudes, aspirations
Work sample or simulation	job tasks, job context, performance standards
Tests/questionnaires	ability, personality, motivation

Other factors in good selection

Accurate assessment criteria do not, in themselves, guarantee reliable and relevant assessments. Other factors would include

❑ relevance and reliability of tools
❑ skilled assessors
❑ appropriate decisions.

It is frequently argued that *relevance and reliability* must be established using statistical analysis of the results obtained from the assessment methods and actual performance in the target job. Where a large number of job-holders already occupy positions for which the selection process is being designed, all assessment methods, including application forms and interviews, should be tested against job performance criteria.

One approach to testing assessment methods is:

1 Use the assessment methods with existing job-holders.
2 Collect ratings of job performance for each job-holder. Where possible, collect 'hard' measures of performance such as targets completed or sales achieved. (Note: at least 50, ideally 100 or more, job-holders are required to complete each assessment method and provide performance ratings.)
3 Scores obtained from the assessment methods are then compared with job performance scores.

The most common statistical analysis used when comparing these types of data is referred to as a test of 'correlation'. Results from this form of analysis are frequently used to report the relationship between assessment methods and job performance – ie how well scores on assessment methods predict scores on job performance. It is often suggested that an assessment method that correlates 0.3 or above with job performance is a useful method. However, there is more to correlation than a single number, and it is meaningless to say 0.3 is good or bad.

We do not cover the subject of statistical analysis of data in this book. We do recommend, though, that anyone in a position to undertake statistical testing of assessment methods should ensure that it is done, and that they have access to expertise in statistical analysis.

Many selection programmes have insufficient numbers of applicants or existing job-holders for statistical analysis to be meaningful. Designing assessment methods based on competencies, job tasks and job outputs can ensure sufficient correspondence between the methods and the job to provide confidence in their relevance. In these circumstances, relevance can be checked by

❏ comparing tasks in assessment exercises with tasks found in the job, to ensure that exercises reflect the job
❏ ensuring that evidence collected when using these exercises with a sample of existing job-holders includes sufficient and relevant examples of the competencies which the exercises were designed to measure.

The *skills of assessors* are an additional and major factor in making reliable and relevant assessments. Assessors need to be skilled in assessing. These skills include the application of particular techniques and rules. Accurate assessment also depends on a thorough understanding of the assessment criteria which include the competencies.

Even with reliable and relevant tools and skilful assessors, accurate assessment requires *appropriate decisions* based on valid rules. This is covered in the section **Making decisions in competency-based assessments** later in this chapter.

Collecting applicant information

Information required to assess applicants for early screening in a selection process is usually collected using an application form.

It is important to consider whether communication of the type required to complete the application form is relevant in the job. For example, not all jobs require a good grasp of the English language. There may be applicants who have the competencies required to do a job but who have difficulty with reading and writing. If the application form is used to screen out these applicants they will not have another opportunity to demonstrate their competencies. Where reading or written communication is not required in the job, alternatives to application forms should be considered. Recruitment-critical competencies should provide a clear indication of the relevance of a written application form for a specific vacancy.

Other methods of collecting applicant information for early screening include:

❑ telephone-based questionnaires, by which applicants are asked questions and for which they use the keypad to provide answers or speak their responses

❑ questionnaires administered via computer, either on a disk or through the Internet.

Whatever the form of collecting applicant information and screening, the process qualifies as an assessment method. As with any assessment method, it should be tested to ensure that it consistently produces relevant assessment evidence.

In addition to general applicant details and information on essential criteria, such as necessary qualifications, these methods can be used to collect competency-based applicant information. This can be done by including a section solely for collecting competency information.

Competency information can be collected in several ways:

❑ open-format questions

❑ a competency-rating questionnaire

❑ a forced-choice questionnaire.

Open-format questions

The open-format approach is best suited to written application forms and requires applicants to provide one or two examples for each job-critical competency. Usually some guidance is given for each competency. For example, to collect information on 'Developing others' ('DEVELOPING THE BUSINESS: Personal development, Level 2') an application form might include the following (obviously with enough space for the applicant to write an answer!):

This job involves developing others. In the space below, please provide two examples of where you have had to manage the development of others. Please ensure that you indicate the issues you dealt with, how you dealt with them, and the results.

Alternatively applicants can be given more of a lead by providing specific questions to answer for each competency. For example:

Developing others

Provide two examples of where you have had to manage the development of others.

What issues did you have to deal with?

What did you do?

What were the outcomes?

These examples are based on the generic behaviours in the competency. At this stage, and with the limited information that can be collected in an application form, it may be more appropriate to use competencies at this level of detail. However, for jobs that require a high degree of experience closely matched to the vacancy, it may be possible to use the more detailed versions of behaviours described earlier.

Competency-rating questionnaires

Competency-rating questionnaires require applicants to rate themselves on statements taken from the behavioural indicators listed within the competency. Behaviours may be rated on a scale to indicate how frequently the applicant uses the behaviour effectively. See, for example, Table 5.

This example has taken behaviours from several competencies and converted them into questionnaire statements.

Just listing behaviours from the competencies will not produce an effective questionnaire because most applicants will

Table 5
COMPETENCY RATING QUESTIONNAIRE

Rate how often you do the following: Key: 1. Usually 2. Often 3. Rarely 4. Never	1	2	3	4
a. account for the impact of your decisions on others				
b. share your learning experiences with colleagues				
c. talk about the achievements of your employer outside of work				
d. identify and seek out information you think you need for your job				
e. etc.				

soon realise that they can present a good image by rating each statement as a '1' or a '2'. It is usual, in questionnaires of this type, to reverse half of the statements so that applicants are required to rate some statements as '3' or '4' to indicate suitability for the vacancy. For example, 'talk about the achievements of your employer outside work' might become 'underplay or avoid talking about achievements of your employer outside work'. This type of questionnaire must be carefully designed and worded so that the behaviours desired by the organisation are not obvious. It must be achieved without making the questionnaire unnecessarily difficult to complete.

Forced-choice questionnaires

The forced-choice questionnaire presents applicants with pairs

---

From each pair of statements choose the statement which describes you better.

a.   Adapts personal style to develop relationships.
b.   Seeks consensus for all decisions.

c.   Presents own views with conviction.
d.   Avoids making decisions which will be unpopular.

e.   Keeps responsibility for decision-making within scope of own role.
f.   Seeks and gives constructive feedback.

g.   Etc.
h.   Etc.

of statements. It is intended that the applicant will believe all statements to be equally desirable from the viewpoint of the recruiting organisation. However, each pair of statements contains a behaviour which is desirable to the organisation and a behaviour which is undesirable to the organisation – each from a different competency. 'Undesirable' behaviours must be relevant to the recruitment-critical competencies so that applicants selecting the behaviours will still be providing information relevant to the vacancy. See the example on page 68.

As with the competency-rating approach, this questionnaire is based on behaviours from the recruitment-critical competencies. In the above example the **Appendix Framework** has been used to develop the statements. Statements *b.*, *d.* and *e.* are negative examples of behaviours from 'WORKING WITH INFORMATION: Decision-making, Level 2'.

Interviews

The interview has been transformed in recent years from the butt of many selection trainers' jokes to a respectable assessment tool. Contrary to popular myths, however, the transformation was not due to the introduction or use of competencies in interviews. Interviews work well when they

❑ are structured
❑ employ clear and relevant criteria
❑ are used by well-trained, skilful and disciplined interviewers.

Interviewers find it easier to stay focused on the appropriate competencies when they use a structure or interviewing guide. This contains guidelines for conducting an interview, such as a structure to follow and information to include in the introduction, along with a clear guide to the questions which might be asked for each competency. The interviewer's skill is used to ensure that sufficient information is collected for all of the competencies included in the interview.

For example, a competency-based interview will seek evidence that the interviewee has employed behaviours like those listed in the competencies. A good interviewer will try to elicit examples of what has been achieved with the behaviours (eg successful outcomes). The good interviewer will also seek to ensure that the interviewee has used the behaviours in appropriate situations – ie that the successes were relevant to a level similar to that of the vacancy.

Competency-based interviews can be as good or as poor as the best or worst interviews.

Oral questionnaires?

A major bank used competency-based interviewing as part of its selection process for customer service staff. More than a hundred staff were recruited using the interview as part of the process. Only accredited interviewers, trained in a very disciplined approach to interviewing, were used to conduct interviews.

Assessment records indicated that very little evidence had actually been collected regarding the competencies during any of the interviews. Further analysis showed that decisions to select or reject a candidate were not based on any of the competencies.

Interviewers had been misguided in how to structure their questions – the process itself did not allow an interviewer the necessary freedom to keep the interview focused on the competencies. In fact, most interviewers were simply reading out each question and noting the reply: no probing or supplementary questions were being asked.

The interview was focused on the right competencies but the supporting materials and training were getting in the way. Retraining and new interview guidelines provided a quick, but necessary, remedy.

Although competencies can contribute to an excellent interview, this example shows that, on their own, they cannot guarantee one.

Apart from the opening and the closing sections of the competency-based interview, the majority of the time requires the interviewee to provide examples of previous performance. Interviewers focus the responses of interviewees using questions drawn directly from the competencies. The competencies explored in an interview should be compatible with the interview process. For example, the interview collects evidence only of reported performance and is therefore not suitable for collecting actual evidence of problem-solving. Problems tackled by the interviewees and their knowledge of problem-solving techniques could be explored during the interview, but assessment exercises which actually test this competency are likely to be more informative.

Questions that might be asked in a competency-based interview include:

WORKING WITH PEOPLE: Influencing
Level 2: Influences the thinking of others

Have you been in situations where you had to influence the thinking of others?

Describe one such situation to me.

What was your role?

What did you do?

Describe how you presented your views.

What outcome were you hoping for?

What was the outcome?

What contribution did others make to the outcome?

An experienced interviewer would not necessarily ask all, or only, these questions and might reword them to complement the responses of the interviewee. Competency-based interview schedules are not scripts to be followed slavishly – they are guidelines to ensure consistency: they provide an agenda or checklist for collecting appropriate examples of competency. Nevertheless, good competency-based interviews have a clear and noticeable structure.

Off-the-shelf tests and questionnaires (psychometrics)

'Off-the-shelf' ability tests and personality questionnaires are frequently used in selection and are often referred to as psychometric tests. The term 'test' usually applies to measures of specific abilities, but this category is often taken to include measures of personality and motivation.

Off-the-shelf psychometric tests are not direct measures of competencies. In Chapter 1, it was shown that characteristics of a person – such as abilities and personality – influence the way the person behaves. Psychometric tests measure some of the characteristics which can influence behaviour – they do not measure how a person behaves when using these characteristics.

If these types of test are to be used in competency-based assessments, it is vital that tests are chosen which will help to screen out individuals who lack characteristics *essential* for performance in the job.

In the car analogy used earlier, tests would tell us about specific characteristics of the car. A garage might, for example, test the power and functioning of a car's brakes, engine and steering. Because these characteristics are important for a car's overall performance, the test results would provide valid information on which to decide whether or not to proceed with further assessment.

Relevant tests might predict aspects of performance but they do not provide evidence of actual behaviour in specific situations. For example, a car may pass the above tests but may behave very poorly when fully loaded at motorway speeds.

Competencies can help to identify relevant tests

In addition to information about skills required in a job, behavioural indicators can provide clues as to whether a test is appropriate in a competency-based assessment. Some tests may closely match several behaviours within a competency; other tests may match only one or two indicators. For example, a test of 'ability to reason with business data' might be closely related to our **Appendix Framework** competency 'Gathering and analysing information: Level 3' (from the 'WORKING WITH INFORMATION' cluster); however, the test may not provide opportunities to assess the indicator 'Identifies new opportunities for the business.'

A selector may choose to use the test for early screening, where there are many applicants, prior to more detailed assessments later in the process. In these circumstances the characteristic being assessed must be an essential characteristic for performance in the job and the test must be a good measure of that characteristic.

When tests count!

A major bank was recruiting graduates for work in foreign exchange roles. The roles laid considerable dependence on numerical skills. An assessment centre had been designed to assess competencies. There were more than 600 applicants for the roles. Sifting by application forms reduced this number to 150. An ability test was designed to measure job-relevant numerical ability and used to further sift applicants down to manageable numbers for the assessment centres.

All candidates attending the assessment centres were able to deal with numerical aspects of the job-simulation exercises. Thus time was not wasted using elaborate assessment centres to measure the competencies of individuals lacking basic skills.

Work sample tests

Another type of ability test with psychometric properties is the 'work sample' test. Such tests are usually designed for a particular recruitment campaign and focus on job-specific activities and can also focus on job-specific competencies. The results from these tests can usually be integrated with other competency assessments, especially when the design is based around the specific competencies relevant to the vacancy.

Testing, testing

A government agency wished to recruit a large number of counter staff. The role involved a great deal of form-filling and checking of forms completed by others. Competencies for these roles included 'attention to detail' and 'following instructions'.

Two tests were devised. The first test involved completing two forms using instructions provided within the test. The second test involved examining different forms which had already been completed in order to identify any errors.

Because there were over 100 existing counter staff, the tests were checked by examining how good performers in the job scored on the tests and how poorer job performers scored. Test scores showed that good job performers scored significantly higher on the tests than poorer performers. The tests were adopted as measures of 'attention to detail' and 'following instructions' and used in the selection process.

Work sample tests do not just copy job tasks. Care is required in the design of these tests and expertise is required to establish rules for scoring. For these reasons, work sample tests are usually developed by experts in psychometric test design.

Simulations

Short of taking applicants on for a few months to 'try them out', a series of work-related exercises would probably provide the most accurate assessment of an applicant's suitability. This would enable applicants to be assessed in realistic situations while undertaking tasks which represent the everyday tasks that the job-holder would be required to perform.

Simulations may sound similar to work sample tests but they differ in important ways. These are illustrated in Table 6.

Table 6
THE DIFFERENCES BETWEEN WORK SAMPLES AND SIMULATIONS

Work samples	Simulations
Single task – eg filling in a form	Several tasks – eg dealing with enquiries
Single competency	Several competencies
Psychometric – ie standardised measures of psychological characteristics	Not usually psychometric
Usually multiple-choice answers or defined range of acceptable answers	Answers not predefined. Behavioural indicators used for assessing answers.
Task is highly constrained	Tasks are broadly defined
An overall score is calculated for the test	A rating is assigned for each competency

Simulations commonly used include:

- in-tray (in-basket) exercises
- group discussions
- role-plays
- case-studies
- presentations.

Ideally, simulations should be based on the job for which individuals are being assessed. In part this is because simulations provide an opportunity to 'test-drive' applicants.

If organisations are going to use simulation exercises, it is likely they will already have a good assessment of the general suitability of candidates before inviting them for assessments based on simulations. This is because simulations usually require more assessor time than other assessment exercises, making them more resource-hungry. However, simulations generally provide the best assessment of candidates' competencies.

Competencies can help to identify relevant simulations

Although vacancy-specific simulations would provide the best 'test-drive', many organisations use off-the-shelf simulations. These are an inevitable compromise between cost/time and quality of assessment. Off-the-shelf simulations can only approximate to an organisation's job activities, required outputs and competencies.

Research has shown that certain types of simulations are better at providing evidence on some competencies than on others. This sort of research makes the choice of simulations easier but it can also mislead recruiters into believing that the specific off-the-shelf simulation(s) they purchase will be suited to their vacancy and their competencies. The research should be used only as a guide. Every assessment exercise should be evaluated to ensure that it provides job-relevant opportunities for candidates to demonstrate the behaviours contained in the recruitment-critical competencies. To ensure this relevance with off-the-shelf simulations it will usually be necessary, at least, to

❑ customise instructions for candidates
❑ rewrite guidelines for assessors
❑ amend the scoring system.

The research can also be used to identify the type of simulations relevant to a vacancy prior to developing vacancy-specific simulations. Table 7 is an example of the extent to which a range of simulation exercises will measure the sample competencies.

Table 7
ASSESSMENT EXERCISES RELEVANT FOR ASSESSING THE APPENDIX FRAMEWORK COMPETENCIES

Competencies \ Exercises	In-tray and de-brief	Group discussion	Case-study	Interview	Fact-finding	Role-play	Oral presentation
Managing relationships	✔		✔	✔✔		✔	
Teamworking		✔✔		✔✔			
Influencing	✔✔	✔✔	✔✔	✔✔	✔✔	✔✔	✔✔
Gathering and analysing information	✔✔	✔	✔✔	✔✔	✔✔	✔✔	✔✔
Decision-making	✔✔	✔	✔✔	✔✔	✔✔	✔✔	✔✔
Developing people	✔			✔✔		✔	
Developing ideas	✔✔	✔✔	✔	✔✔			
Planning	✔✔		✔	✔✔			
Achieving outcomes	✔✔	✔✔		✔✔		✔	
Objective-setting	✔✔	✔✔	✔✔	✔✔		✔✔	

✔✔ – competencies most frequently observed in exercises of this type
✔ – competencies frequently observed in exercises of this type

This example (based on the IPD *Tools for Assessment and Development Centres*) indicates the types of exercises which might be used for assessing our **Appendix Framework** competencies. The actual content of the simulation exercises would need to be identified and the number of exercises used would usually be restricted by practical constraints – eg time, costs and numbers of candidates.

To ensure that simulations provide a comprehensive and reliable assessment of all recruitment-critical competencies it is normal to use several simulations in a single assessment. After producing a grid of simulations that could be used, such as the one above, the following rules would be applied to refine the matrix:

❑ Each competency should be measured at least twice.

❑ Avoid designing simulations in which poor performance on one competency would make it very difficult to demonstrate effective performance on other competencies within the same exercise. For example, do not try to assess 'objective-setting' and 'planning' together because agreeing to poor objectives may make planning to achieve them impossible.

❑ No single simulation should measure more than five competencies (ideally three).

❑ Simulations should provide appropriate opportunity for competencies to be demonstrated equally by all candidates.

This approach to identifying which simulations will be used is very common but it is not necessarily the most effective. Not all types of simulations apply to all jobs. Because they are also limited in number there is a danger that selection processes include certain simulations only because they provide an opportunity to measure certain competencies, not because the activity simulated is found in the job.

Stand up and be counted

A call centre was recruiting staff to answer customer enquiries over the telephone. One of the essential competencies was identified as 'influencing others', and one of the exercises designed to assess this competency was a 10-minute presentation. Candidates were asked to prepare for this when they were invited to the selection interview.

Many candidates did not do well on this exercise because their presentation skills were not developed enough to allow their influencing skills to come to the fore. Because influencing through presentation was not part of the job, this exercise was actually hindering the selection process. In addition, the type of influencing that *was* required in the job was not being assessed.

Designing simulations for specific vacancies

A more focused yet less restricted way of identifying potential simulations is to match the competencies required in a job to key tasks which are to be performed in the job. In this way simulations can be developed which are unique to the vacancy.

Competencies provide one of the measures for identifying a simulation for a particular vacancy. For example, in our

Appendix Framework competencies the behaviours listed under 'Changes the opinions of others' ('WORKING WITH PEOPLE: Influencing, Level 3') could be assessed using an exercise which simulates a negotiation or meeting where the outcomes will affect other people. The focus of the meeting and the types of people involved would need to be identified using additional information about the vacancy – eg typical issues tackled and types of situations which typically require influencing.

Here is an example of how vacancy-specific simulations could be identified:

1   Identify the key tasks which job-holders will be required to undertake – eg producing sales reports, co-ordinating project teams, conducting performance reviews, making presentations.

2   Identify the recruitment-critical competencies or competency levels.

3   Produce a matrix of the competency levels and the key tasks.

4   Indicate which competencies/levels are critical for which key tasks by placing ticks in the matrix.

An example of the type of matrix that this process produces is shown in Table 8.

The matrix is then refined in the same way as for generic simulations described earlier – that is, each competency should be measured at least twice, etc.

Each column in the matrix in Table 8 can then be used to develop specific exercises. It may not be necessary to develop an exercise for each column – for example, it may be possible to measure all competencies at least twice using four or five exercises. Sometimes it is also possible to combine tasks in one exercise: internal post and report writing, for instance, could be combined in a business-reporting exercise.

To ensure that competency-specific evidence is collected using simulations, the simulations must be designed in a way that provides individuals with opportunities to demonstrate the competencies.

Prompts for examples of competencies can be built into:

Table 8

MATRIX SHOWING THE RELATIONSHIP BETWEEN COMPETENCY LEVELS AND KEY JOB TASKS

Key job tasks / Competency levels	Drafting project plans	Internal post	Team meeting	Project meeting	Project work	Meeting with clients	Staff mgmt meeting	Sales presentation
Builds relationships externally				✔		✔		✔
Supports team members			✔				✔	
Influences the thinking of others						✔		✔
Checks and analyses information		✔			✔	✔		✔
Ensures that decisions are made		✔		✔			✔	✔
Develops others			✔		✔			
Develops ideas into solutions	✔	✔		✔		✔	✔	✔
Plans to meet departmental objectives	✔				✔		✔	
Manages resources effectively	✔	✔		✔	✔			
Sets responsibilities			✔	✔		✔	✔	

❏ the instructions given to candidates
❏ the exercise activity
❏ the outputs requested from the exercise.

For example, assuming that four competency levels have been identified for assessment using a sales presentation exercise, the matrix shown in Table 9 could be used to ensure that relevant competencies are prompted by the design of the exercise.

Using the matrix in Table 9, the designer of the assessment simulation exercise considers how the competency level on the left might be stimulated in the way in which the exercise is

Table 9

MATRIX FOR INCORPORATING COMPETENCIES INTO A SALES PRESENTATION EXERCISE

Competency levels	Briefing the candidate	Exercise activity	Outputs required
Builds relationships externally			
Influences the thinking of others			
Ensures that decisions are made			
Develops ideas into solutions			

written. For example, the competency level 'Develops ideas into solutions' could be stimulated by ensuring that the briefing to the candidate clearly indicates that the presentation should include a solution based on previously-developed ideas. These ideas can be included in material given to the candidate for the exercise.

The designer reviews each of the competency levels and considers at which point in the exercise it will be most appropriate to stimulate the competency. Notes on how the behaviour can be prompted are written into the relevant cells

---

A picture paints a thousand words

A public utility was designing a selection process for civil engineering supervisors. The job involved a number of key activities including safety checks at building sites.

Simulations were designed around each of the key activities. For example, one simulation provided candidates with photographs of actual work sites. In this simulation the photographs contained a variety of good and poor safe working practices. Candidates were asked to report their observations and recommendations using brief notes – the same form of reporting that would be required in the job.

All the simulations were reviewed by existing supervisors and trade union representatives. The simulations were unanimously endorsed as representative of the vacancies, and full support was given to their use and the decisions made when using them.

of the matrix. When all competency levels have been reviewed, the notes in the cells of the matrix will provide a draft for the exercise.

The process is completed for each key task until all competencies can be assessed at least twice

Identifying the key outputs which job-holders will be expected to produce – eg levels of sales, new project developments or staff management – can help in exercise design. As indicated above, exercises can be designed to prompt candidates to produce outputs similar to those which would be required in the job.

Assessment centres for selection

An assessment centre, although often presented as an assessment tool or technique, is actually a process. The process uses a combination of some or all of the assessment exercises described above. What makes it different from other selection processes (which may also use a combination of the above exercises) is the way in which it is organised. In fact, it is better described as a Multiple Assessment Process (MAP) in which there are:

❑ multiple participants
❑ multiple assessors
❑ multiple exercises
❑ multiple criteria.

To maximise objectivity, the MAP programme is organised so that every participant does every exercise and is seen/assessed at least once by every assessor.

The points made in this chapter regarding the contributions which competencies can make to selection processes also apply to assessment centres.

Making decisions in competency-based assessments

Evaluating evidence of competency requires clear and unambiguous decision rules. It is essential that these rules are set up before decisions begin to be made in order to prevent unfair biases from creeping into the decisions. Ad hoc changes to decision rules late in the process will reduce the consistency and accuracy of selection decisions. As with any form of selection, decision rules should be tested before they are used in order to ensure that they provide effective and fair discrimination between candidates.

An important consideration for any assessment process is that decisions should be both reliable and relevant to the vacancy.

Assessment decision rules are defined before selection commences and are applied after evidence of candidate competency has been collected. In competency-based selection these decisions usually apply to:

❑ turning evidence into assessment ratings
❑ combining ratings from different exercises
❑ turning ratings into accept/reject decisions.

Turning evidence into ratings

Rating scales are normally used to assign ratings to evidence of competency. In selection, the rating scale can be short because evaluation usually focuses on evidence of acceptable or unacceptable competency. Typically, scales range from three rating-points to five rating-points; only one scale should be used throughout the process. Examples of scales are shown below:

1. Acceptable	1. Fully meets the standard	5. Outstanding
2. Marginal	2. Acceptable	4. Good
3. Unacceptable	3. Marginal	3. Acceptable
	4. Poor	2. Marginal
		1. Unacceptable

The more scale-points there are, the easier it will be to refine decisions about who should proceed to the next stage of selection. For example, the four-point scale allows for a decision rule such as 'Applicants who obtain a rating of one on all competencies will progress to the next stage, followed by applicants who achieve ratings of one and two with a majority of one ratings,' and so on.

Scale-points must be both meaningful and justified – eg 'acceptable' must be defined in terms of the evidence sought for the competency, and this should correspond with acceptable application of the competency in the target job. The definition of 'acceptable' may have been established during the original competency analysis or when identifying recruitment-critical competencies.

The first point in selection where applicants might be rejected or accepted for further assessment usually occurs following receipt of applicant information – eg application forms. Short-listing at this stage is not primarily about matching applicants against competencies. Criteria which would restrict or bar applicants from doing the job should be reviewed first – eg a requirement to work overseas or a legal requirement to hold a professional or technical qualification. Competency information is used if applicants pass these requirements. There is little point in spending time evaluating the competency evidence of applicants who do not meet the more basic requirements.

The primary task of the assessor is to match reported behaviour (eg from application forms or interviews) or observed behaviour (eg from tests or simulations) to examples of behaviour in the recruitment-critical competencies.

Competency ratings are produced in two ways:

❑ converting scores from tests and questionnaires
❑ comparing written evidence with behavioural indicators.

Converting scores from tests and questionnaires

Competency-based questionnaires, such as those used for applications, are relatively straightforward because competency scores can be related directly to ratings. The rules for doing this are usually established when the questionnaire is trialled. For example, trialling might indicate that poor performers usually score between 0 and 3 on the questionnaire for a particular competency, while good performers usually score between 11 and 15 for that competency. Table 10 provides an example of rules that can be compiled for converting scores to ratings. It is worth noting that different tables may be required for each competency because good performers may, for example, produce scores in a different range on each competency.

Table 10

EXAMPLE OF CONVERTING COMPETENCY SCORES TO COMPETENCY RATINGS

Questionnaire score	Competency rating
0–3	4
4–10	3
11–15	2
16–20	1

Scores obtained from psychometric tests and questionnaires can also be converted using the approach shown in Table 10. However, there are some complications, because psychometric tests and questionnaires

❑ do not usually provide direct measures of competencies

Diagnosing differences

A pharmaceutical company ran a series of internal assessment centres which used simulations and ability tests. It was noticed that candidates occasionally scored well on numerical reasoning tests but were not rated highly on competencies where analysing numerical information was important. This was creating a lot of discussion among assessors because they were having difficulty trying to assign an overall competency rating for 'analytical reasoning' based on low competency ratings from exercises and high ratings from the test.

Because the assessment centre was internal it was possible to follow-up the differences between test performance and competency ratings with individuals. It was established that individuals who performed well on the test but not on the competency required additional skills to put their numerical reasoning ability (as measured in the test) into practice with work-based tasks.

Following this finding it was decided to continue to use tests but not to integrate them with ratings of competency. Test scores were used to identify potential which could be realised through targeted development.

❏ often contribute to more than one competency.

If scores from these measures are to be used to produce competency ratings, the relationship between scores and competencies must be established. This is a challenging task best left to experts.

Alternatively, and as preferred by the authors, scores from these measures can be left out of the overall competency assessment. Scores can then be used to interpret the overall assessment.

Comparing written evidence with behavioural indicators

Assessment evidence will be in the form of written notes. Notes will be provided by the applicant – as in open-format application forms or written output from an exercise – or produced by assessors when observing or interviewing the candidate.

Assessors read through the written evidence from a particular assessment method. The pieces of evidence are then classified, using behavioural indicators, into the competencies for which the exercise was designed. The quality and volume of the evidence per competency is then translated to a competency rating. Table 11 provides an example of rules that can be compiled for converting written evidence to ratings.

Table 11
EXAMPLE OF CONVERTING WRITTEN EVIDENCE TO COMPETENCY RATINGS

Evidence	Rating
Multiple effective examples of all behaviours with no negative examples	1. Outstanding
	2. Good
Effective examples of most behaviours with no negative examples and no important omissions	3. Acceptable
	4. Marginal
Multiple negative examples of behaviours with no positive examples and/or with important omissions	5. Unacceptable

Note that in Table 11 only the first, third and fifth rating-points have been defined. This makes the assigning of ratings much easier for assessors and reduces the incidence of split ratings: eg 2/3 and 3/4 or 3+ and 3–.

There is a significant difference between evaluating application evidence and evidence collected using other methods. Generic behaviours may be more appropriate for evaluating application evidence due to the limited information that can be collected. Evidence from other assessment methods can be evaluated using more detailed vacancy-specific behaviours.

Combining scores

In the case of selection processes which use a combination of assessment methods/exercises, there will be more than one rating for each competency. There are two key ways in which scores are usually combined to produce a single rating for each competency. One method is to average the ratings obtained for each competency. Alternatively, assessors discuss the evidence for each competency rating and reach consensus on an overall rating for each competency.

The latter can be more meaningful because differences between ratings for a competency can be explored. For example, high and low ratings may have been given for a particular competency. On exploring the evidence behind each rating it may emerge that the higher ratings were too lenient. Assessors may therefore assign an overall competency rating lower than that which would be obtained by averaging.

The consensus approach also has the advantages that

❑ overall ratings are whole numbers
❑ the development needs of individuals are often identified during these discussions
❑ the discussions can be used to prepare for feedback.

The overall rating could be based on the same rating rules used for allocating individual competency ratings within exercises. For example, Table 11 could be used to assign individual and overall competency ratings.

It is essential that assessors are trained in how to combine scores to produce a single rating for each competency.

It is only when a single rating has been produced for all

competencies that assessors move on to decision-making.

Turning scores into decisions

Rules are applied to overall competency ratings to identify which applicants are to pass on to the next stage of selection. Selectors need these rules to ensure a consistent approach when interpreting sets of competency ratings. Rules may be different at different stages in the selection process, but it is important that they are established and agreed before the recruitment process is implemented.

As with the definitions of rating-points, decision rules should be meaningful in terms of job performance. For example, if it is essential that a job-holder demonstrates acceptable-to-outstanding performance in all the competencies, the rules must reflect this.

Different decision rules may apply where applicants are being screened following receipt of applications and where candidates are being accepted or rejected following more detailed assessments. Rules used at the application stage are likely to be more lenient than rules applied after extensive assessments because information available at the application stage is limited.

Rules for short-listing applicants should be set by comparing scores obtained by existing job-holders with how well the job-holders are rated in terms of other job performance criteria. The approach may require large numbers of job-holders to establish that these rules actually relate to different levels of job performance. Expertise is required to establish these rules.

Table 12 shows a set of rules which could be used for open-format applications where, for example, four competencies are investigated.

Table 12
EXAMPLE OF RULES USED TO RATE APPLICATION FORMS WITH FOUR COMPETENCIES

Fail	Applicants rated '1' on any competency or more than two '2's
Reserve	One or two ratings of '2'
Recommend	Two or three ratings of '3'
Pass	Three or four ratings of '4'

In this example the rules would be applied in top-down order – ie 'fail' applicants are identified and removed from the applicant list. Next the 'reserve' applicants are identified, followed by 'recommends'. This will leave the 'pass' applicants. If there is a quota for passing applicants to the next stage and the number of applicants who 'pass' falls short, then high-scoring 'recommends' might be added to the 'pass' list, followed by lower-scoring 'recommends'. If the quota is still short, the higher performers on the 'reserve' list could be added.

Table 13 is an example set of rules which might be used after detailed assessment of applicants (based on a five-point scale).

Table 13
EXAMPLE OF RULES FOR USE AFTER DETAILED ASSESSMENT

Accept candidates who obtain … *Accept rules are applied in order, moving down the opposite column, until the target number of candidates have been accepted. If applying these rules does not produce a sufficient number of recruits then top up using the 'hold' rules.*	all '1's; mostly '1's and '2's on others; mostly '1's and '2's with a few '3's; all '2's; mostly '2's and '3's with a few '1's; mostly '3's with a few '1's '2's; all '3's.
Hold candidates who would be acceptable but for … *If 'hold' candidates are required for the recruitment quota, individual candidates should be selected in order of the 'accept' rules (in the order above right) plus the one or two '4's rule – eg first select candidates with all '1's except for one or two '4's; next select candidates with mostly '1's and '2's with one or two '4's; and so on.*	one or two '4's.
Reject candidates who obtain … *Rejected candidates must not be upgraded to 'accept'.*	more than two '4's and/or any '5's.

Competency-based assessment feedback

The competency ratings and evidence of competency from different assessment methods can be used to follow up with candidates after selection decisions have been made.

Unsuccessful candidates could be given feedback based on

examples of evidence against each competency. Unsuccessful candidates usually find it easier to relate their performance to assessment methods and therefore prefer feedback to be given based on the methods. Overall performance feedback can be given based on competencies such that examples focus more on the assessment methods.

Successful candidates may be provided with more detailed feedback of their performance and may benefit more from feedback about performance on specific competencies. Feedback can form part of a development action plan as well as highlighting areas of strength.

In either case, the competencies enable feedback to be based on words rather than numbers. The words can be drawn directly from the behavioural indicators and used to compare what was sought with what was observed. Feedback based on observations of performance against competencies helps avoid making the feedback too personal and encourages a more accepting and positive atmosphere.

Using competencies to monitor selection

Competencies can play a useful role when monitoring the decisions and actions taken during selection. Records of selection decisions and ratings of competency, if regularly reviewed and acted upon, can help organisations to improve their selection processes by

❑ preventing unfair selection decisions
❑ maintaining, or improving, the effectiveness of selection decisions.

Records of the ratings which individual applicants received against competencies can be used to assess:

❑ fairness – eg how assessors assign ratings to evidence
❑ how well individuals who received high scores on competencies subsequently performed, using these competencies, in the job.

In addition, retaining examples of competency provided by candidates on each assessment method will assist in reviewing the effectiveness of the methods. This information will help reviewers to check that the range of behaviour which the methods were expected to generate has actually been observed and recorded.

In brief

Selection seeks to establish a match between people and the demands of work before placing them in a job or role. This match is affected by a wide range of factors, and the best match requires that as many of these factors as possible are assessed before making a selection decision. In assessment terms, it is necessary to find out what people can do and how they go about doing it. It is also important to ensure that they can do these things in circumstances similar to those which will be found in the job or role.

The selection process therefore relies on a wide range of information. A variety of tools is necessary to collect this information, and skill is required in use of the tools and use of the information.

Behavioural criteria, such as competencies, provide support throughout the selection process. Competencies indicate necessary behaviours for performing a job effectively. Competencies provide a structure for collecting behavioural information and can assist in the design of tools for collecting this information. At the end of the selection process, competencies can be used for feeding back assessments to candidates, and they provide a set of criteria for monitoring the effectiveness of the selection process.

The overall effectiveness of a selection process does not depend solely on competencies. It takes more than the introduction of competencies to a selection process to improve selection decisions. The quality and relevance of assessment exercises, rating scales, decision rules, the selection process and the quality of assessors' skills are critical factors in the overall quality of selection decisions.

Use of the term 'competency-based selection' overemphasises the importance of competencies and tends to take attention away from the other critical factors. Currently, selection processes are drifting toward a primary focus on competencies. Indeed, many sophisticated selection processes, including assessment centres, now assess only competencies. Yet a thorough assessment of performance must take account of how well an individual completes work-relevant activities as well as how he or she goes about those activities.

For many organisations, improved selection may be more easily and more quickly achieved if greater attention is given to using selection exercises and processes that are better matched to the job and by investing more time and effort into the training of assessors.

Further Reading

PEARN KANDOLA (1996) *Tools for Assessment and Development Centres*. London, Institute of Personnel and Development.

4 USING COMPETENCIES TO REVIEW PERFORMANCE

In this chapter, reviewing performance is seen as a part of performance management processes and refers to *all* situations in which the performance of an individual is reviewed, not just appraisal interviews. Reviewing performance might be a self-review or it could involve one or more others. This chapter does not include acting on outcomes from the review. Addressing under-performance and enhancing performance are dealt with in the chapter on development and training (Chapter 5).

Performance reviews require skill to do well, and they require tools to help manage the process – eg for collecting and structuring information.

The purpose of reviewing performance

There are many reasons for the performance of job-holders to be reviewed. From an organisational point of view these include:

- managing poor performance (ie identifying training and development needs for the current role)
- motivating staff (eg setting challenging and stretching objectives and providing positive feedback)
- rewarding good performance (either through pay or some other reward)
- reinforcing stated organisational values and culture

❏ identifying training and development needs for future roles
❏ succession-planning (identifying individuals capable of moving to other jobs in the future)
❏ auditing (finding out what strengths and development needs exist in the organisation).

From an individual's point of view these include:

❏ identifying how well the individual is performing in his or her job or role
❏ identifying training and development needs for the current role
❏ rating performance for reward
❏ identifying potential to move on to another role.

In summary, performance reviews – while addressing many of the above needs – focus on one or more of the following purposes:

❏ establishing levels of performance
❏ identifying needs for performance improvement
❏ identifying development potential for succession
❏ discussing career interests/direction.

What constitutes a performance review?

Performance reviews are usually part of a larger process (eg appraisal and career planning). These larger processes frequently begin with setting objectives and action plans based on the requirements of the job and the abilities and development needs of the job-holder. The process then continues with interim reviews which monitor and revise action plans – in the form either of modified objectives or of a training and/or development plan. The process usually culminates in a formal review or appraisal of performance against both the objectives and the action plans.

Typically, performance reviews take place as one-to-one discussions between a job-holder and his or her manager or supervisor. However, reviews can also be conducted by teams or as a solo activity.

Increasing emphasis on teamwork has resulted in moves to

review team performance as well as, or instead of, individual performance. Empowered teams may well be left to manage themselves in relation to who does what and how – a major measure of success being the achievement of team-set targets.

Whatever form the review takes, it will usually contain feedback on a job-holder's performance. It may be against pre-set objectives, behaviours and/or action plans. This may involve performance feedback from a range of people, from the job-holder to his or her manager, peers, direct reports and customers.

The contribution of competencies to reviewing performance

Competencies can make significant contributions to each of the purposes listed earlier, ie:

❏ establishing levels of performance
❏ identifying needs for performance improvement
❏ identifying development potential for succession
❏ discussing career interests/direction.

These contributions can clearly be seen in the steps which all performance reviews appear to have in common. No matter how complex or simple the review process, all forms of reviews usually follow a similar structure:

❏ identifying factors relevant to performance in the job
❏ collecting information on performance
❏ organising the information
❏ discussing or reviewing (eg for solo reviews) the information
❏ agreeing outcomes.

Identifying factors relevant to performance in the job

Once in the job, an individual will have specific things that he or she must achieve – ie targets or objectives – and these may contain (we would argue that they *should* contain) specific and measurable outcomes. These outcomes are one type of job-performance measure: ie they are measurable indications of a job-holder's progress towards fulfilling the purpose of the job.

A performance review might focus only on how well an individual has progressed toward meeting his or her targets or objectives. The more specific and measurable an objective or target, the easier it is to review that aspect of the performance of a job-holder.

However, performance is no longer seen just as 'what' a job holder achieves (eg quantity targets, such as the number of units produced, items sold or calls answered). Job performance is seen also to be about 'how' the job is carried out (eg the behaviour exhibited by the job-holder). Many organisations now review both what is achieved and how it is achieved when assessing job performance.

You get what you reward

Several years ago, a major international company expressed concern about poor relationships between one of its subsidiary companies and its partners abroad. One of the main objectives of the subsidiary company was to guide the marketing of its parent company's key products in international markets.

Within the subsidiary company all customer-facing sales and marketing staff were set performance targets based on sales volumes. Individuals were then appraised and rewarded according to performance against these targets. Sales met their target but customer complaints were rising and customer satisfaction (ie satisfaction of its international partners) was plunging. Job-holder performance was reviewed only at annual appraisals in which the main focus was on assessing outputs and setting new output targets. Everything was aimed at short-term gains (outputs) without concern for how those gains were achieved, to such an extent that the future of the sales and marketing company was at risk.

In contrast, a public-sector organisation replaced its traditional appraisal process with a performance-review process based solely on competencies. This was founded on the belief that if a person does things in the 'right' way, they must produce the right outcomes. At first this might seem quite logical. However, competencies do not explicitly state what has to be done, nor do they define responsibilities or expected outcomes. Focusing performance reviews only on competencies (inputs) left individuals without clear direction, and disagreements arose about tasks and responsibilities.

These examples illustrate that problems can arise when performance reviews take too narrow a view of performance. Narrow views of performance inevitably lead to an underestimation of factors relating to or influencing job performance. This in turn undermines the potential benefits of reviewing performance by, for example, placing too much emphasis on either the 'how' or 'what' aspects of performance.

Unlike coming up for selection, the individual is now in the job, and this means that a lot more information is available, potentially, to help review an individual's performance. For example, a job-holder could be reviewed against all aspects of his or her job, such as:

❑ producing things (eg products or decisions)
❑ fulfilling responsibilities (eg the management of others)
❑ behaving in a way that is acceptable within the organisation
❑ operating within particular contexts and environments
❑ dealing with other people
❑ operating pieces of equipment
❑ operating processes and procedures.

Although it might be possible to collect performance information on each of these areas, it is more usual to summarise performance into just two areas: the achievement of objectives, and behavioural performance. Competencies can be used to develop part of this picture of performance. Behavioural performance information can be collected using direct evidence of competency, ratings of competency or feedback on competency observed by those close to the job.

At this stage in the process (identifying factors relevant to performance), competencies can provide a structure for collecting evidence of behavioural performance. So it is necessary to identify the competencies and the levels of competency (if relevant) that are required in the job being reviewed.

Restricting the collection of competency performance information to competencies critical to performance at the required level reduces both time and effort in collecting the information. This restriction also makes it easier to maintain a focus on important behavioural performance during the review discussion.

One way of identifying critical competencies or competency levels is to use a process similar to that used for identifying recruitment-critical competencies. For example:

1 List the most critical job tasks required to meet the job purpose.
2 List the competencies (or competency levels) that would be required to undertake each of these tasks.
3 Rank these competencies (levels) in order of their importance to completing the tasks.

Another approach that can be very effective is called 'paired comparisons'. This approach provides a more accurate assessment of importance. With this approach, competencies are scored according to their relevance to each key task or activity. To do this, each competency is compared in turn with every other competency, identifying which is the more important in each pairing for achieving the task or activity. In this way, scores for the importance of each of the competencies for every task or activity can be produced. There is insufficient space here to describe the approach fully, but many books on problem-solving techniques describe this in detail, and a brief example is included in **Appendix 2**.

These steps can be undertaken with existing job-holders and/or their managers because these individuals should have the most realistic view of the job. In many cases it is likely that job-critical competencies will have been identified during the production of the competency framework or later if selection against competencies was used to fill job/role vacancies.

Finally, it is important to be sure about the purpose of the performance review. For example, if a review is to assist in discussions about careers, the focus may be on competencies for future roles. However, reviews to establish levels of performance usually focus on competencies required in a current job/role.

Collecting information on performance

Once the competencies have been identified, there is a number of ways in which information on behavioural performance can be collected.

The three basic forms of information that can be collected are:

- ratings of performance
- comments on performance
- examples of performance.

The type of information collected is likely to vary according to the availability of performance information and the purpose of the review. For example, many organisations use ratings of performance only where an overall performance rating is being sought as the outcome of the review – eg for pay reviews. However, other organisations collect comments only where the review purpose is to increase an individual's understanding of how he or she is perceived by others. Where an individual is new to a role, some organisations request individuals to undertake job-relevant assignments and to provide examples of outputs from the assignments.

Another way of collecting evidence of competency performance, widely used by many organisations, is to use an assessment centre process. This is justifiable for assessing competency performance for future or significantly changing roles. However, it is hard to justify using such a process to review performance relative to an individual's existing role – unless the normal performance management and review process has not been used effectively, or where there are significant barriers to collecting on-the-job performance information. These assessment centres are often referred to as 'development centres', but this is an inaccurate description because the primary purpose is to assess performance and, by so doing, to assess individuals' development needs. We prefer to call this type of process an 'assessment-for-development centre' and it is covered later in this chapter.

Assessment centres are discussed in the selection chapter (Chapter 3) and development centres are discussed in the chapter on training and development (Chapter 5).

Effective performance management and performance reviews should avoid the need to conduct assessments of an individual's competency performance using assessment centre processes. If a person is already doing the job, then collect information directly from the job using one, or a combination, of the following techniques:

- questionnaires

❏ records of achievement
❏ assignments
❏ assessment-for-development centres.

To review performance relative to future roles or for career planning, the previous techniques may provide necessary information – but this could be supplemented with information from:

❏ an assessment centre (looking at future roles)
❏ career review exercises.

Table 14 lists the different types of information and methods of collection that may be used for different reviews.

Collecting information using questionnaires

Questionnaires can be used to collect ratings of competency performance and they can also be used for collecting

Table 14
EXAMPLE OF TYPES OF INFORMATION AND METHODS OF COLLECTION USED FOR DIFFERENT REVIEWS

Purpose of review	Forms of information	Method of collection
To establish level of performance (current role)	Behavioural performance Output performance Task performance	Questionnaires, records of achievements, observations.
To identify need for performance improvement	Behavioural performance Output performance Task performance Personal circumstances Organisational issues	Questionnaires, records of achievements, observations, discussions (eg with job-holder)
To identify development potential (future role)	Behavioural performance Output performance Task performance	Assessment centre, assignments
To discuss career interests	Work history Competency profile Aspirations Interests, knowledge and abilities Opportunities	Assessment centre, development centre, discussions with individual

comments on competency performance. It is not always the case, however, that one questionnaire will collect both ratings and comments. Different questionnaires may be used to collect, for example,

- ratings against each behavioural indicator
- ratings against each behavioural indicator plus comments
- ratings against each competency
- comments on competency performance plus ratings against each competency
- comments on competency performance.

Because questionnaires are to be used to collect performance information about real job-holders in real jobs, the ideal questionnaires will be developed from the competencies necessary for effective performance in that job. Where an organisation has developed a competency framework, it should provide the basis for developing the questionnaire.

In addition, many organisations use 'off-the-shelf' competency questionnaires. These can offer a great deal of convenience where an organisation does not have a competency framework or where the framework does not cover the group of roles for which feedback is needed.

Features of off-the shelf questionnaires include:

- They are readily available.
- They are often machine-scoreable.
- Some provide comparisons with ratings obtained in other organisations.
- They provide professional-looking reports.

But where a competency framework does exist, off-the-shelf questionnaires can pose problems. Matters that should be resolved when considering the use of such questionnaires include:

- Do they reflect the organisation's values/culture?
- Will they undermine confidence in the existing competency framework?
- Will users be distracted or confused by having more than one framework in use?

❏ What ownership will people feel for the content of the questionnaire?

The two main types of questionnaire used for collecting competency feedback, off-the-shelf or purpose-designed, are

❏ ratings-based
❏ comments-based.

In the ratings-based type of questionnaire, raters are asked to rate each indicator of each competency rather than give an overall rating for each competency. For this questionnaire an overall rating is calculated for a competency by combining the ratings of the competency's indicators. It is therefore important that the questionnaire enables raters to provide their best estimate of a job-holder's behavioural performance. This can be made easier by providing questionnaires that contain job-specific examples of the behavioural indicators – ie statements which describe how each behaviour would be observed in the particular job or role.

This type of questionnaire is often used where an overall rating of performance is being sought or a profile of the job-holder's competencies is being developed.

The indicators-based questionnaire can include sections for written comments, although they can make the questionnaire lengthy. If comments are particularly important, an alternative is to use a questionnaire in which the primary purpose is to collect written comments for each competency.

Competency-based performance reviews are not always undertaken to produce an evaluation or profile of a reviewee's competencies or for appraisal. Another purpose is to provide the reviewee with insight into how he or she is seen by others. Although ratings-based questionnaires can be used for providing this feedback, it can be much more powerful when there are specific examples to illustrate why colleagues have given particular ratings.

It can be useful to collect an overall rating for each competency with this questionnaire because comments alone can be misleading.

The addition of a rating helps to ensure that comments are considered in the context of a view of overall competency. Without the rating there is a danger that positive or negative

> ### Who said that?
>
> Foreign exchange dealers in a major international bank attended a series of development workshops. During these workshops they were observed undertaking job-relevant tasks and they also received feedback on the tasks as well as feedback from competency questionnaires completed by colleagues. Dealers frequently challenged observations of performance fed back by assessors. However, they readily accepted observations from their colleagues, taken from questionnaires, even though these simply confirmed the assessors' observations.

comments will be over-interpreted. Over-interpretation is especially likely where individuals in completing a questionnaire provide only one or two comments to highlight what they consider to be important issues.

When developing or choosing a questionnaire, careful consideration should be given to both the design of the questionnaire and its implementation. In particular, consideration should be given to

- the length of the questionnaire
- its structure
- its rating scale
- who will complete the questionnaire
- managing the volume of questionnaires.

The length of the questionnaire

Years of experience have shown that most people do not like long questionnaires. It is therefore not a good idea to produce one questionnaire that includes all the behaviours in the competency framework. Many of the behaviours will not be relevant for specific job-holders being reviewed and will waste time and distract raters.

Different jobs will have different competency profiles, so consideration must be given to producing job- or role-specific questionnaires. Where it is important that the review includes a detailed examination of competencies and/or where detailed behavioural indicators already exist, a job-specific questionnaire may be justified. An alternative is to develop role-specific questionnaires – eg one for supervisory roles, one for administration roles, and one for middle-managerial roles.

One way of producing job- or role-specific questionnaires is to organise the generic competency framework in a database or in word-processing files. The framework should be organised so that relevant job or role profiles can be printed out in a format appropriate for use in a questionnaire. For example, each competency level could be stored as a record in a database. It is then relatively easy to produce a job- or role-specific questionnaire by creating a file of behavioural indicators which correspond to the competency levels in the job or role profile.

Another effective approach is to administer the questionnaire on the computer screen. This can be done directly from a database. An advantage of this approach is that responses can be manipulated by the computer to produce feedback reports for the review discussion.

Automatic cover

A life assurance company introduced performance reviews for its sales staff. To facilitate the reviews a handbook was produced which included pencil-and-paper-based questionnaires and guidance for the review process.

After successful use of the handbook, the process was computerised. This enabled feedback questionnaires to be administered from the computer and for development profiles to be easily and automatically analysed.

The structure of the computer program enables updating of the competencies, and completely new competencies can easily be added. Because the computer contains the whole competency framework, new job-specific questionnaires are easily compiled.

Structure

Questionnaires are often designed in such a way that raters cannot easily tell which areas of performance specific questions relate to. However, in a competency framework some behavioural indicators (which will be converted into behavioural questions for the questionnaire) may be easier to interpret if it is evident which competency they relate to – for example, if behavioural questions are grouped under the relevant competency heading.

We have found that the most consistent ratings of competency for review are achieved when questionnaires are structured so that raters can clearly see which competency each indicator relates to.

Rating scale

Behavioural indicators are often rated using scales which require raters to indicate how effective they think the job-holder has been at using each of the behaviours, or how frequently the job-holder has used the behaviours effectively. Actual scales may vary depending on the specific application. For example, a major insurance company featured two scales in the same questionnaire – the first to indicate the frequency with which behaviours were used when needed, and the second to indicate how effective they were when used.

Because some raters may not have an opportunity to observe all behaviours listed in the questionnaire, it is important that raters are able to respond 'cannot say' where appropriate. Each point of the rating scale must be clearly defined and definitions should be kept as simple as possible.

Tables 15 and 16 give two examples of rating scales.

In Table 16 (example 2), raters are asked to use both scales to rate each behaviour. This approach enables more accurate ratings than Table 15.

Who will complete the questionnaire?

Questionnaires for performance reviews should be completed by individuals best placed to provide accurate feedback – ie those individuals with whom the job-holder's job requires regular interaction. When several people are asked to complete questionnaires relating to one reviewee it is called a 'multi-rater' (sometimes alternatively called a 360-degree) process.

Recent research indicates that multi-rater feedback can be affected by how confident the rater is that his or her feedback is going to remain anonymous. Perhaps it is not surprising that when raters believe they might be identified as the source of a low rating they tend to moderate their feedback scores. In

Table 15

EXAMPLE 1 OF A RATING SCALE FOR PERFORMANCE REVIEW

Use the following scale to indicate how often and how effectively the person used each of the behaviours listed in the questionnaire:	
5 Cannot say	You have not been present in situations when the person needed to use the behaviour
4 Very effective	The person used the behaviour effectively whenever a situation needed it.
3 Moderate effectiveness	The person used the behaviour in most situations which needed it and it was usually effective.
2 Marginal effectiveness	The behaviour was not very often used in situations which needed it, and/or when it was used it was not usually effective.
1 Poor effectiveness	The behaviour was not used in situations which needed it. Or if it was used, it was not effective.

Table 16

EXAMPLE 2 OF A RATING SCALE FOR PERFORMANCE REVIEW

Use the following scales to indicate how often and how effectively the person used each of the behaviours listed in the questionnaire:			
Rating	**Frequency of use**	**Rating**	**Effectiveness**
5	No opportunity to observe		
4	All occasions when it was needed	4	Always effective
3	Most occasions when it was needed	3	Usually effective
2	Very few occasions when it was needed	2	Occasionally effective
1	Never, even though situations needed it	1	Never used effectively

general, this finding does not apply to the job-holder's manager, who in many feedback systems will be easy to identify. It has also been reported that job-holders tend to be more lenient when they rate themselves. However, we have found that this varies, depending on the purpose of the review. Where the review has a clear development purpose, job-holders often *underrate* their own performance.

Collecting feedback from several colleagues is more effective when it is reserved for special situations – for example, a development event or career review – or at least limited to the annual performance review. The job-holder is often left to choose whom he or she would like to complete questionnaires, and for development events this has proved very effective because individuals often choose to apply for feedback from those who will not hide their opinions. A self-completion is almost always included, and other completions would include those of direct reports, peers, the manager and significant others. Significant others have included customers and professional colleagues from outside the organisation. The number of questionnaires to be completed varies from one to more than 12. Including self-completion, seven to nine completed questionnaires is usually sufficient.

Questionnaires can also provide job-holders with a useful 'one-off' tool for self-review or for collecting the views of one or two individuals to review specific situations, such as individual roles within a project, or difficulties with particular working relationships.

Managing the volume of questionnaires

Competency questionnaires completed by several colleagues can produce a powerful review tool, but the tool can be weakened if the approach is used too often or if individuals do not have sufficient time to complete the questionnaires. In organisations where appraisals are scheduled within a narrow time-period, staff can get overloaded with requests for providing review feedback because each individual may have several roles:

❑ job-holder
❑ peer to several colleagues
❑ manager
❑ internal supplier
❑ internal customer

❑ project team member.

Not only does this mean that an individual could be asked to complete ten or more questionnaires, it also means there could be ten times as many questionnaires in circulation than numbers of staff. If all appraisals are happening within an annual pay review period, these questionnaires will be distributed and will be circulating during a very short time-period. Add to this issues of confidentiality while keeping track of which questionnaires have been completed and it becomes clear that a process is needed to manage distribution and collection of questionnaires.

Computer-based questionnaires can alleviate the administrative load provided that confidentiality is built into the questionnaire. Yet a tracking system of some description will still be necessary to enable the chasing up of tardy respondents.

Collecting information using records of achievement

For many years trainee and apprenticeship schemes have included records of achievement as part of the review of an individual's technical and skill development. These records, maintained by the job-holder, contain specific examples of work done by that individual. National Vocational Qualifications (NVQ) and Scottish Vocational Qualifications (SVQ) schemes also include this type of performance record. During the last five years organisations have begun to extend the use of the record of achievement to include examples of behavioural performance for a wide range of staff. These examples may be actual outputs – eg copies of letters or reports – or they may be written summaries of how the individual has dealt with specific situations relevant to the job competencies – ie the behaviours.

It is important, however, when using records of achievement, to train both the assessors and the people collecting the information. Individuals must be aware of the type of information required, and the quality. This will reduce the chances of collecting huge volumes of relatively useless paperwork.

This material lends itself to a wide range of performance reviews – for example, solo reviews of performance, discussion with peers or team, or review with manager and/or mentor.

It's quality, not quantity, that counts

In one public-sector organisation, records of achievement were introduced. The training required the staff to be briefed about what sort of information would be needed. Three months later an assessor was presented with a file 80mm (slightly more than 3 inches) thick – full of paperwork to back up one competency.

The training was then amended to cover quality. As a visual demonstration two files were held up. One 80mm thick and the other a much slimmer 16mm thick (less than three-quarters of an inch). The trainer announced that both files contained enough information to assess the same competency – and for everyone concerned the thinner file was the preferred one.

Collecting information using assignments

An assignment is a work-based project or task designed to allow an individual to demonstrate his or her competencies in relevant circumstances. Assignments can be useful for reviewing performance against current or future roles. They are used for current roles when an individual

❑ has not been in a job long enough to obtain work examples
❑ is taking, or has taken, on new responsibilities
❑ has had mixed feedback about performance in a particular area of the job.

Because competencies overlap in their importance with key elements of jobs, most assignments enable the collection of information on more than one competency.

Assignments must be carefully specified to ensure that tasks within them are representative of the job being reviewed and that these tasks provide adequate opportunities for observing and recording competency-relevant behaviours.

Individuals who undertake assignments can be given guidelines for the recording of behaviours, the approach, and the outcomes during the assignment. Interpretation of the behaviours, approach and outcomes may be done solo, using written guidelines, or it could be reviewed in a team setting, or a one-to-one setting.

Collecting information using assessment-for-development centres (ADCs)

The purpose of an ADC is to identify what an individual would have to learn, or to improve on, to be considered a suitable candidate for another job. Assessment centres for selection were covered in the selection chapter (Chapter 3). Centres which are based on assessment centres but which do not result in competency scores, and which are primarily for participants to practise and get feedback on competencies, are development centres, which are covered in the training and development chapter (Chapter 5).

ADCs are usually events during which individuals undertake a number of assessment activities. An individual's performance in each activity is compared against a benchmark. This comparison results in a profile which is fed back to the individual. The outcome of the ADC process is usually an action plan which addresses those areas in which the individual's performance fell short of the benchmark. To retain the distinction between assessment centres for selection and those for identifying development needs, we will refer to the latter as ADCs for the remainder of this chapter.

Competency frameworks can be used as

❏ an aid in the design of the ADC activities
❏ the benchmark against which performance is measured
❏ the framework for discussing outcomes with the individual.

These points are expanded below.

There are two things that can be done to improve the contribution which competencies make to the design of ADCs:

1   Identify the competencies or competency levels which are *critical* for effective performance in the target job or group of jobs. This will minimise the total number of competencies to be observed. Six to eight essential competencies are usually sufficient – and will usually be the same as, or closely linked to, those chosen for selection purposes.

2   Identify detailed examples of the generic behavioural indicators – ie what these generic behaviours actually look like in the target job or group of jobs.

Guidelines on how to undertake these steps can be found in the selection chapter (Chapter 3).

ADC activities are essentially the same as assessment activities for selection – that is, they allow observers to assess the levels of performance in an activity against the benchmarks agreed. The principles of the design of such activities are also similar to those outlined in the selection chapter (Chapter 3) and we do not propose to repeat them here. However, there are some important differences between the events that surround ADCs and those that surround assessment centres for selection. These are:

❑ benchmarking
❑ feedback.

In much the same way that they can be adapted for use in selection events, behavioural statements can be used in ADCs. However, it is likely that a wider range of acceptable behaviours will be used – especially in cases where people are attending an ADC to assess potential for another job or level in the organisation.

Another key difference between assessment centres for selection and ADCs is the emphasis on feedback during and after the development event. In many ADCs the feedback is extensive and focuses on what was observed rather than ratings of performance.

Organising the information

Following the indicator-based questionnaire approach, the overall score for each competency is calculated for each questionnaire (rater) before ratings from all questionnaires are combined to produce the feedback information. 'Cannot say' ratings should not be incorporated into the overall competency rating. 'Cannot say' ratings should be reported separately in the feedback because these can be useful pieces of information – especially if they are ratings given by people who *should* be able to say!

When competency scores are collected from a group of colleagues (such as peers, direct reports and line manager), it is a relatively easy task to combine and analyse scores on each competency. This information can then be fed back graphically, as in bar charts, and it is easy to feed back comparisons of scores – eg how colleagues rated a reviewee on a competency and how his or her direct reports rated him or her on the

Figure 3
ILLUSTRATION OF SCORES USING A BAR CHART

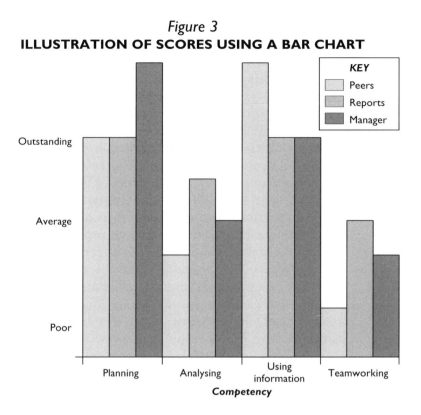

Competency

competency. Figure 3 is an example of how scores can be illustrated using a bar chart.

Such a diagram is a useful presentation of competency ratings because it enables easy comparison between groups of raters, making it easy to identify significant differences between them. This is important because significant differences can occur when groups rate a competency, and these differences may be quite valid and meaningful. For example, direct reports may have the best opportunities and experiences to provide the most accurate ratings of their manager's 'developing others' competency. A job-holder's manager may be in the best position to rate the job-holder on 'converting organisational plans into departmental plans'.

A separate overall rating can also be presented for each competency. Presenting this separately and in addition to ratings from the different rater groups reduces the potential to discard meaningful differences. Such differences can be lost if overall competency ratings only are produced. For example, a job-holder may have received an overall average rating for 'teamworking'. On surveying the ratings from different rating groups it may appear that peers and more senior colleagues have rated the individual at a little above average whereas members of the team that the individual manages have given consistently low ratings. This difference could be critical, indicating that the individual's approach to working with his or her team's members is below an acceptable standard.

Some competency-based feedback systems go much further and present a breakdown of ratings. This breakdown usually gives some indication of the spread of ratings obtained within each competency and within each rater group. Table 17 shows how this may be presented.

In this example there are nine raters, as indicated in the top row. For each competency the highest and lowest ratings are shown for each group of raters. This level of detail is useful when there is a dispute over the overall rating given to a competency. For example, it may be that direct reports tend to see a different side of their manager's 'leadership style' than do the manager's colleagues. This detail is also useful when diagnosing performance and when considering development. These points are covered later in this chapter and also in the chapter on the use of competencies in development (see Chapter 5).

A similar format can be used to summarise ratings by rater groups at the behavioural indicator level. At this more detailed level, the range of ratings can be displayed, as in Table 17, and the number of 'cannot say' ratings can also be included. In practice, having both overall competency ratings and detailed

Table 17

EXAMPLE OF SPREAD OF RATINGS PER COMPETENCY

Raters / Competency	4 x Reports		3 x Colleagues		1 x Manager		Self	
	min	*max*	*min*	*max*	*min*	*max*	*min*	*max*
Managing relationships	3	4	2	5	3	3	4	4
Teamworking	4	4	3	3	3	3	4	4
etc								

indicator ratings makes it easier to prepare rating information for the review discussion.

Where examples of performance have been collected – eg records of achievement and assignments – they are usually evaluated – eg rated – against the competencies before they are discussed. Rating guidelines are required to do this consistently.

Examples from ADCs will usually be evaluated at the centre by the facilitators. Assignments and records of achievement may also be evaluated prior to the review discussion. These could be evaluated by the job-holder, if trained to do so, or by some other trained person. The important thing with this type of information is not to reduce it to a number (rating) which, compared to the examples, is relatively meaningless. It is the examples that are important because they indicate the elements of a competency that may require training or development. If a person has been rated '3' overall for 'Planning', it may indicate that the person has a development need in this competency. Another person may be rated the same but have a different development need in that competency. What is important for the review discussion is *why* the person was rated as having a development need. A good reviewer will have prepared evidence from the available examples to support his or her assessments of competency.

When preparing feedback from questionnaires, the reviewer also needs to prepare examples to illustrate ratings. In the comments-type questionnaire, examples can be selected from the comments to illustrate consistent themes: both strengths and development needs. Examples can even be prepared from the rating questionnaire. In this case preparation may focus on ratings of the behavioural indicators. Where a competency received an overall poor rating, it is important that the reviewer can quickly show which behaviours contributed to the poor rating – ie which behaviours were rated lowest – and, if appropriate, which rater groups rated them low.

Reviews should be balanced. Preparation should ensure that individuals are aware of potential strengths as well as development needs. Preparation must not just seek examples to reinforce feedback of weaknesses or development needs.

> ### One step forward, two steps back
>
> A grant organisation ran a series of ADCs to assess the potential of staff for supervisory positions. The feedback from the ADCs was focused entirely on development needs. Unfortunately, this meant that participants felt deflated, hearing only messages about what they were not yet able to do – ie were not good at. The result was that instead of leaving the ADC looking forward to developing into a role, most participants left feeling that they would never make it.

Discussing the information

Performance review discussions require skill and good preparation. The reviewer should be someone who has a good understanding of both the purpose of the review and the review information, which will often contain information in addition to that on competency.

Where a review follows an assessment centre for selection or an ADC, it is usually better if the review discussion is undertaken by a centre facilitator because he or she will be intimately acquainted with the examples of performance. If reviews are based on questionnaire feedback prepared on behalf of the reviewer, the reviewer must then spend sufficient time getting to understand the information before the review discussion.

Just because rating type information is easier to present does not mean that it is easier to discuss. Rating information, usually in the form of multi-rater feedback, is becoming very popular. This may be because

- it is easy to work with the data
- analysis of data is not as time-consuming as analysis of written information
- it is easy to present the information graphically.

Drawbacks to this form of feedback are that:

- this form of feedback may appear more factual than is warranted
- raters will not have had equal opportunities to observe all behaviours

❏ behaviours may not be equally amenable to rating
❏ the reviewee focuses more on the scores than on the examples.

These points must be borne in mind and accounted for during the discussion. It may be that during the discussion examples are explored which result in changes to evaluations arrived at when preparing for the discussion.

As stated earlier, job performance is not just about outputs, nor is it just about behaviours or competencies. A thorough and meaningful performance review should also look at factors which impact on an individual's ability to demonstrate appropriate behaviours, and factors that influence the individual's ability to deliver the required job outputs. These factors relate to characteristics of the person and their personal circumstances as well as circumstances within the organisation and its characteristics. The relevance of specific personal and organisational factors to performance usually becomes apparent only once behavioural and output performance has been established. It is therefore usually during the discussion of performance information that these factors are identified and explored.

Performance reviews which do not take account of these personal and organisational factors tend to place too much responsibility for performance on the individual.

There are many factors which influence how job-holders behave and perform. Table 18 lists a number of these factors.

There are a few important points that reviewers need to keep in mind when feeding back a summary of competency ratings:

❏ It is easy for this form of review information to appear, or to be presented, as a series of facts – eg 'You are good at this' … 'You are not so good at this.' This should be avoided.
❏ The feedback summary is a very structured and condensed set of perceptions. It is not a definitive statement about the reviewee.
❏ It is quite feasible that some behaviours have been misinterpreted by raters.
❏ This form of review information is for discussion. It is a tool to check out the reviewee's view of his or her typical competency.

Table 18

EXAMPLES OF FACTORS THAT CAN INFLUENCE PERFORMANCE AT WORK

Factor	Examples
Domestic	❏ home life – ie family role, relationship issues ❏ other commitments – eg hobbies, studies, voluntary work
Organisational	❏ resources for work ❏ politics at work ❏ context – eg changes, uncertainty ❏ relationships ❏ culture ❏ role/task clarity
Managerial	❏ relationship ❏ support for the job ❏ support for the person ❏ changes
Personal	❏ abilities – mental and physical ❏ preferences ❏ values ❏ traits ❏ experience ❏ knowledge ❏ attitudes

❏ The examination of examples provided in discussion by the reviewee may result in a new view of the reviewee's competency.

❏ Disagreements between groups of raters can be meaningful. It can be useful to explore disagreements during the review to develop an understanding about how they may have arisen.

❏ Behaviours may not be equally amenable to rating. Some behaviours, such as those related to analysing information and decision-making, may not be easy for some colleagues

– who may see only superficial aspects of some behaviours – to rate.

One example of this in our **Appendix Framework** is the behaviour 'Decisions made when appropriate with limited information' ('WORKING WITH INFORMATION: Decision making, Level 3'). Many observers may have knowledge of the decisions a reviewee has made, but few (if any) may have been close enough to know what information was used and what information was available.

These points reinforce the need to use competency rating feedback as a basis for a discussion about the behavioural side of performance rather than as an assessment tool.

Solo/self-review

Not all performance reviews are conducted with another person or other people. It is possible for individuals to review performance information alone. If individuals are going to undertake solo/self-review, there should be very clear guidelines to assist them through this process. The important points that reviewers need to keep in mind when feeding back information about competency ratings outlined above are particularly relevant here. If there is no one with whom an individual can discuss the outcomes, it may be easy for review information to be seen as 'the final word' rather than as a basis for exploring behaviour.

On the whole, performance review is better conducted with at least one other person, if only so that an alternative viewpoint or challenges can be put forward. Solo or self-reviews can, however, be beneficial in their own right, as well as helping individuals to prepare for discussion with others.

Agreeing outcomes

If assessment – ie an overall rating – of the behavioural performance of an individual is required, it should result from a discussion of the questionnaire feedback – it should not come directly from questionnaires.

Annual performance reviews and appraisals usually feature an overall performance rating. Including competencies in the review process automatically raises the perceived importance of behaviour in job performance. As illustrated in the earlier example **You get what you reward**, ignoring competencies when producing an overall performance rating reduces the perceived importance of behaviour.

A thorough assessment of performance therefore includes evaluations of both competency performance and achievement of outputs, taking account of both personal and organisational influences. Such an assessment often results in ratings for achievement of each output as well as ratings for each competency, especially when the review contributes to pay awards. This approach is often taken further to produce an overall rating for achievement of outputs and an overall rating of competency performance. Although these overall ratings may be kept separate, a third stage is sometimes included which integrates ratings of achievement of outputs and competency performance to produce a combined performance rating.

This approach results in three layers of ratings:

❑ individual ratings for competencies and for outputs
❑ overall rating for competencies and for outputs
❑ overall performance rating.

For example:

❑ an individual has been rated on six targets and eight competencies
❑ rating scales similar to those in Table 19 are then used to establish an overall rating for outputs and an overall rating for competencies
❑ the two overall ratings are then combined to produce one overall performance rating.

Combining performance ratings

Organisations combine overall output and competency ratings in different ways. Three examples are:

1 Average the two overall ratings.
2 Produce an average after weighting one of the overall ratings: eg some organisations give more weight to outputs than to competencies.
3 Use a set of rules to limit the combined rating – eg to avoid

Table 19
EXAMPLE OF RATING SCALES

	Outputs	Competencies
5	Exceed standards required on all targets	All competencies rated 'outstanding'
4	All targets achieved to required standard: some exceeded	A mix of 'good' and 'outstanding' ratings
3	Most targets achieved to required standard	Most competencies rated 'good'
2	Many targets achieved close to standard; a few not met, but progress made	Most competencies rated 'marginal'
1	Very few or no targets achieved to standard	Most competencies rated 'poor'

a very low rating and a very high rating being averaged to produce a mid-level combined rating.

In the first example (average of ratings) an overall output rating of '5' and an overall competency rating of '3' would produce a combined rating of '4'.

In the second example an overall output rating might be weighted by a factor of 2. So an overall output rating of '5' and an overall competency rating of '3' would produce a combined rating of '6.5' (5×2 [the weight] = 10, 10 + 3 [the competency rating] = 13, 13/2 = 6.5).

These approaches can produce odd combined scores. For example, the first approach would produce a combined rating of '3' for overall ratings of '1' and '5'. The definition of a combined rating of '3' may be 'acceptable'. However, the organisation may consider that anyone obtaining a rating of '1' cannot be considered acceptable.

The effect is less exaggerated with the second approach. For example, a rating of '1' on outputs and a rating of '5' for competency would produce a combined rating of '3.5'. However, the total scale for combined ratings using this approach is 7.5 to 1.5, whereas for the first approach the scale is 5 to 1.

Table 20
COMBINING OVERALL RATINGS

Overall ratings	Combined rating
5 + 5	5 – outstanding
5 + 3, 5 + 4, 4 + 4	4 – good
5 + 2, 4 + 3, 3 + 3	3 – acceptable
5 + 1, 4 + 2, 4 + 1, 3 + 2, 2 + 2	2 – poor
3 + 1, 2 + 1, 1 + 1	1 – unacceptable

In the third example a set of rules may be applied to recognise the presence of low ratings. Table 20 illustrates how ratings could be combined.

This approach produces a combined rating of 2 for overall ratings of '1' and '5', acknowledging that overall performance is considered poor.

In brief

Performance reviews may be undertaken for a wide variety of purposes, and to be effective they must focus on what an individual does (outputs); how he or she does it (behaviour), and the factors that may influence these things (personal and organisational factors). Reviews that focus on limited information do not produce a fair view of overall performance. Where used for reward, limited reviews are likely to encourage individuals to adopt a narrow view of what is important in their work.

Competencies provide a useful focus for obtaining information on behavioural performance which, although important, is only one aspect of performance. Behavioural performance or competency information can be generated in many ways and collected from a variety of people. The collection process requires specialist tools and effective procedures to manage the volumes of both information and work that can be generated.

Care must be taken when using competency information because questionnaire data, in particular, can be easy both to misinterpret and to misrepresent. To be meaningful the data must be discussed in the light of what the person is trying to achieve as well as personal and organisational influences.

Competencies also provide a useful structure for feeding back or discussing behavioural performance. It is important when preparing information for a review discussion that the information is not reduced to simplistic numbers. Where ratings of behavioural performance are discussed, it is important that the purpose of the review is not forgotten. In many cases the purpose will be to ascertain the level of an individual's performance and to identify areas for improvement. The purpose is not to discuss behavioural performance: it is to use such a discussion to arrive at the overall view of performance, which then leads to some form of action – eg a development plan or a pay adjustment.

A good review requires a good reviewer – someone who can effectively prepare performance information for a review discussion, evaluate the information against benchmarks such as competencies and measurable targets, apply rating rules, explore (with the reviewee) any personal and/or organisational factors that may be affecting performance, integrate output and behavioural information with personal and organisational factors, and arrive at a fair assessment of overall performance. This is someone who is well trained and experienced.

Although competencies can make important contributions to performance reviews, the use of competencies does not make performance reviews more effective than the use of any other behavioural criteria. There are many other factors which can impact on the effectiveness of a review. All of these are important.

5 USING COMPETENCIES FOR TRAINING AND DEVELOPMENT

In this chapter we treat training as an aspect of development. We present 'training' as encompassing activities and events which concentrate on the learning and practice of specific techniques. We consider 'development' to be much broader and something that takes learning on to the development of skill and expertise.

This can be illustrated as follows:

'Training' and 'Development'

Joe decides that he needs to learn to drive. He takes a series of formal lessons with a driving instructor. He also goes out, with his mother (who is an experienced driver), to practise in between his lessons. Joe passes his driving test at the first attempt.

Taking driving lessons and practising is Joe's 'training' – he learns and practises specific techniques. The fact that Joe has passed his test does not mean he is a skilful driver. It does mean that he was able to demonstrate that he understood, and could put in to practice, the techniques required to drive a car safely.

Over the following years Joe 'developed' his driving skills and expertise. He did this by applying the techniques he had been trained in to a whole range of different conditions and circumstances. Because he learned from his experiences, he became a skilful driver.

The purposes of training and development

There are many reasons for training and development to be seen as important from both the organisation and individual perspectives. These reasons include the need for

❑ people to stay employable throughout a lifetime during which jobs and careers may change – *a willingness to continue learning and developing is becoming an essential part of continuous employability*

❑ employees to learn methods and techniques required to do specific tasks – *eg people who are new to a job, people having to use new equipment, processes and procedures*

❑ the development of future successors – *minimising the costs of recruiting externally and maximising the benefits of keeping in-house knowledge and experience in the business*

❑ increasing resources from existing staff – *increasing the capacity of people in the organisation to be skilled in more than one area*

❑ motivating, attracting and retaining key staff – *as fragmenting of the workforce (eg with the use of outsourcing and contract staff) continues, and as fewer people join the job market each year.*

Training and development therefore usually serve one or both of the following purposes in the pursuit of a successful organisation or career:

❑ to ensure that techniques and skills meet current needs

❑ to ensure that techniques and skills are prepared to meet future needs.

Factors that influence training and development

Training and development provided by an organisation

Factors that influence the training and development offered within an organisation include:

❑ organisational strategic plans – in particular any changes from current levels or types of business

❑ organisational policies – which may include the provision of events to identify needs (eg assessment-for-development centres) and/or a policy of encouraging learning *per se*.

❑ career opportunities available within the function (eg support for progression within a profession through nationally recognised qualifications) or within the organisation (eg support for progression within the internal hierarchy through generic training such as in management techniques)

❑ future needs – the need to develop staff towards other roles (succession) or the need to develop staff to meet changes in the business (eg the introduction of new technology or an attempt to change culture)

❑ skills shortage – ie the skills of the current staff do not meet current requirements

❑ the need, or desire, to meet external requirements – to gain recognition of a commitment to training (eg Investors In People), to comply with legal and/or professional regulations (eg the Personal Investment Authority or Control Of Substances Hazardous to Health) or to secure funding (eg via Training and Enterprise Councils for National or Scottish Vocational Qualifications).

The aims of training cause many companies to take positive action to ensure that their staff are given opportunities to train and develop. As we can see above, however, there are many factors that influence what those opportunities are.

Training and development realised by an individual

The factors that influence how much learning *actually* takes place are environmental and individual.

Environmental influences include:

❑ availability of resources, both in terms of the number of people who can be 'released' at any one time to attend an event and in terms of the amount of budget available to pay for the events

❑ quality of the event – how formal or informal, structured or unstructured, events meet the objectives of the learner

❑ quality of post-event support – the level of support in helping the learner transfer learning in the workplace

❏ learning culture – how much an organisation promotes learning by seeing mistakes as learning events to encourage people to avoid mistakes in the future through positive action rather than as subversive action.

Individual influences include:

❏ learning styles, preferences for different types of learning activity and previous experience of what works best for the individual

❏ motivation, based on the positive and negative reinforcements of what is accepted behaviour in the organisation

❏ personal needs – for example, the ambition to learn to improve one's employment prospects, either within the organisation or outside it

❏ personal interests, based on what the person enjoys doing or wants to do to challenge himself or herself

❏ personal situation (ie what else is on the individual's mind) – personal circumstances may affect how well an individual can concentrate

❏ potential/current knowledge – eg does the person have the underpinning knowledge required as a prerequisite for the learning?

❏ abilities – is the person able, intellectually, to grasp the theories, concepts and so on that are being trained? And does the person have the manual dexterity needed to be trained in certain tasks?

These lists, although not definitive, show that however much training and development is offered and is taken up, the actual learning that takes place is influenced by many different factors.

The contribution of competencies to training and development

Training is usually undertaken because of a lack of technical ability. That is, training usually addresses competence based on work outputs and tasks. In addition, training usually addresses technical competence for a specific purpose – eg presentation skills training, selection interview training, appraisal interview training and keyboard skills training. The use of the term 'skills' is somewhat misleading here because individuals are not trained in skills, they are actually trained in techniques. Training does not make someone skilful – skill is developed with the practised application of the techniques (remember the driving analogy at the start of this chapter).

A competency is the result of the skilful application of several techniques in combination with particular attitudes, values, abilities and knowledge. For example, successful team leading can be the result of effective training in such techniques as appraisal interviewing, management of meetings, feedback or performance management. But it also relies on, among other things, an interest in developing people, respect for individuals' needs, knowledge of the team members, and personal motivation to do a good job.

The narrow focus of 'technical' training suggests that training related to competencies must focus on elements smaller than the competency by

❏ identifying underlying elements to the competency that can be developed through training – eg techniques or knowledge gaps
❏ focusing training at the behaviours, where these lend themselves to training methods.

For example, in our **Appendix Framework** there is a competency called 'Decision-making' (part of the 'WORKING WITH INFORMATION' cluster). Underlying elements of Level 1 of the competency may include training in such techniques as decision-making, procedures, authority limits, who to refer certain decisions to, and so on. It may also include training in behaviours such as how to search for information and how to refer decisions appropriately.

Focusing on underlying elements and on the behaviours required of a competency are valid approaches to training and development. However, there are other training and development activities that can be undertaken by concentrating on the competency as a whole. These would allow all of the individual's knowledge, attitudes, values, abilities, and so on, to be brought together and practised – for example, a development activity that allowed someone to practise making day-to-day decisions in a realistic or actual work situation.

Competencies provide a framework for training and development that applies to all these three approaches (techniques, behaviour and whole competency) in that they can assist in:

❑ the objective review of training and development needs
❑ the design of training and development activities
❑ the selection of an appropriate training and development activity
❑ the evaluation of activities to ensure that they are in line with the original training and development needs and the organisation strategy
❑ monitoring progress towards a training and/or development goal.

An objective review of training and development needs

There are several ways in which training and development needs can be recognised. They include:

❑ performance reviews, formal and informal
❑ multi-rater/360-degree reviews
❑ assessment exercises for selection
❑ assessment exercises for development
❑ self-review
❑ career-development interviews.

Whatever system is used, the basic principle remains the same. Identification of training and development needs involves the comparison of a set of requirements for successful performance in a job against the personal performance of an individual – either one who is in the job or one who would like to be. To put it another way: it is about reviewing an individual's performance against a benchmark.

It is important to know whether a need is a training one or a development one. This may seem like splitting hairs, but it is an important difference. The question that needs to be asked is 'Assuming that he or she is *able* to undertake the activity, does the individual *know* what is required to undertake it?' If the answer is 'No', it is likely to be a (technique) training need. If the answer is 'Yes', it is likely to be a (skills) development need. For example, if people are poor at 'deadline management', it may not be because they haven't been on the requisite 'time management' course, but because they are not taking responsibility for ensuring that commitments are met.

Most of the above methods of identifying training and development needs have been covered in either the selection chapter (assessment for selection: Chapter 3) or the performance review chapter (performance reviews, multi-rater reviews, assessment for development and self-reviews: Chapter 4). Career-development interviews are slightly different in that they may be as much to do with finding appropriate benchmarks as they are to do with comparing performance against them.

Career-development interviews

A career-development interview is a structured discussion between an individual and another person about the individual's aspirations and prospects. We use the term 'career' to mean the progression of an individual from job to job in a way that will maximise current competencies and open up opportunities to develop competencies which will be useful in the future. This is perhaps a departure from previous definitions, which put the emphasis on promotion through a company or profession, because a career may involve several sideways moves and changes in profession or sector.

Many people conduct career-development interviews, including

❑ training and development specialists
❑ mentors
❑ line managers
❑ external consultants
❑ outplacement consultants.

The key factor is that each of these people has a broad knowledge of other jobs either within the organisation or externally. They may or may not have knowledge of the person who has sought advice.

Career-development interviews in the past commonly focused on interests, qualifications and experience. And this – particularly in interviews conducted by people not experienced in career development – may be unnecessarily restrictive when it comes to discussing options.

For example, Susan has the following experience, qualifications and interests:

Experience:	Qualifications:	Interests:
❑ four years in a large accountancy firm ❑ two years in accountancy department in a high-street bank	❑ professional accountancy qualification (ACA) ❑ five GCSEs ❑ two A-levels	❑ netball ❑ football ❑ reading

An inexperienced counsellor might be tempted to focus on the accountancy experience, and Susan's career choices might then be limited to searching for the 'right' type of job within accountancy. This could, for example, be one which has structured hours to allow Susan time to get to her sporting practices and fixtures. Although these are valid opportunities, focusing on the above factors alone could be limiting Susan's career choices unnecessarily.

Competencies can add an important dimension to the career-development interview. For example, Susan has identified, through recent attendance on an assessment-for-development centre, that she excels in the following competencies:

❑ Teamworking (Level 3).

❑ Gathering and analysing information (Level 2).

❑ Planning (Level 2).

❑ Deadline management (Level 2).

❑ Generating and building on ideas (Level 1).

Building these into the career-development interview may lead to a wider range of job opportunities. For example, the list may broaden to encompass jobs which are not necessarily in accountancy but which draw on Susan's team management skills.

People conducting well-rounded career-development

interviews therefore need information about the individual's competency profile. This can be obtained by means of:

- ❏ performance reviews, formal and informal
- ❏ multi-rater reviews
- ❏ assessment exercises for selection
- ❏ assessment exercises for development
- ❏ self-review
- ❏ questionnaires.

Any information gained through these methods must be viewed with certain factors in mind:

- ❏ How objective is the information? That is, is it self-reported or the result of input from others observing the individual's behaviour?
- ❏ How broad-ranging is the information? Assessment exercises for selection or development are likely to have restricted the competencies to those essential for the target job or level and are therefore likely to have left out other competencies in the framework.
- ❏ For what purpose was the information gathered? For example, selection events will concentrate on performance against prescribed benchmarks, and feedback may therefore not contain detail about which level of competence was reached.

Whatever the event that preceded the career-development interview, the outcome of the interview is the identification of training and development needs, and suggestions about how to meet those needs. This is covered in a later section of this chapter.

The design of training and development events

Training events encompass any activity in which an individual learns something new. Development events encompass any activity in which learning is put to practice in such a way as to develop skill and expertise. Table 21 illustrates what some of these activities might be.

The less structured, more informal activities (mostly development events) are, by their nature, not 'designed' as such.

Table 21
EXAMPLES OF STRUCTURED AND UNSTRUCTURED TRAINING AND DEVELOPMENT EVENTS

Training events	Development events
❏ courses/classes ❏ seminars ❏ lectures ❏ workshops ❏ distance learning ❏ on-the-job learning (taking instruction while doing the job)	❏ trying something different ❏ observation of, or discussions with, a more experienced person ❏ project work ❏ secondments to another area ❏ simulation exercises/assignments ❏ team-building exercises

However, many of the points that we make below could equally be applied to both structured/formal and unstructured/informal activities. For the purposes of clarification we will use the term 'event' to describe the teaching element (which is, from the participant's point of view, more reactive) and the term 'activity' to describe the learning element (which is, from the participant's point of view, more proactive). An event is likely to include, or be followed by, activities. An activity, however, does not have to be instigated or preceded by an event.

While there are many different ways of designing training and development events, designers usually have to take into account

❏ the learning objectives of the participants, team, department and/or organisation

❏ current competency levels of the participants

❏ situation(s) in which the learning will be put into practice

❏ available training expertise, internally or externally

❏ available resources (eg money, time, materials and space).

With the exception of the available resources, competency frameworks can help in all of these considerations.

Learning objectives

The reason a training and development event is designed in the first place is that there is seen to be a need: either an individual need or a group need. It is obviously important that the event focuses on meeting that need, but events are not always successful because although the focus of the event may be right, the context may not.

Running out of time

A major financial institution was running training in telephone techniques for its customer service staff. The course focused very much on the customer service element of the calls. However, the customer service objectives of the course were never fully met because the event neglected to train these techniques in the high-pressure, high-turnaround requirements of the real day-to-day situation. Staff simply didn't have time to ask customers if they had fully understood what had just been said, or to ask if there was anything else they could help the customer with, because they were under pressure to answer as many calls in each hour as they could.

At both an organisation and a departmental/section level there may be requirements to improve certain competencies. A competency framework will assist in establishing the learning objectives of events designed to help address such shortfalls. This is because the required behaviours of individuals who are performing successfully at a certain level of competency are already known. For example, there may be a requirement to improve team leadership skills in an organisation or department. Reference to the competency framework will give an indication of what behaviours are required to demonstrate successful team leadership skills. In the **Appendix Framework**, ('WORKING WITH PEOPLE: Teamworking, Level 3') these would be:

❑ Uses knowledge of individuals' strengths, interests and development needs to delegate tasks.
❑ Provides regular feedback to the team.
❑ Ensures that team members understand their individual and collective responsibilities.

And because the **Appendix Framework** is structured on an incremental basis (ie competency at one level assumes competency at all previous levels), the behaviours for Levels 1 and 2 would apply as well.

The more specific the framework to the situation, the more closely-matched learning objectives based on behavioural indicators will be. If, however, a generic framework is being used, some work will need to be done to ensure that behaviours are relevant and put in context. How to do this is covered in the chapter on producing a competency framework (Chapter 2).

The learning objectives of individuals are covered in the section on the evaluation of training and development activities later in this chapter.

Current competency level of participants

Although an event is designed to meet certain learning objectives, the current competency level of participants will help structure the material. Material that is too complex or too simple will quickly 'turn off' participants, however well presented it is.

Ways of finding out competency levels of event participants include:

- pre-event questionnaires for participants and/or line managers
- performance ratings
- a skills audit
- personal knowledge of participants.

Competency frameworks can assist in finding out current levels of competency, mostly by providing a framework for questionnaires and audits.

The primary purpose of a pre-event questionnaire is to establish what level the participant in a training or development event has reached. It is likely to include questions about the participant's knowledge and experience. The questionnaire can be structured around the competencies covered in the event. Table 22 is an example of a pre-event questionnaire for an Influencing Techniques course based on our **Appendix Framework** 'WORKING WITH PEOPLE: Influencing' competency at Level 2.

The results of this questionnaire can give the person who is delivering the event a feel for where there is a need to concentrate his or her efforts. It may be that one or two particular

Table 22
EXAMPLE OF PRE-EVENT QUESTIONNAIRE

Listed below are a number of behaviours related to influencing. Review each behaviour, and rate how frequently you feel your normal behaviour matches the description, using the rating scale shown.					
1 – always 2 – often 3 – sometimes **4 – rarely 5 – never**	**1**	**2**	**3**	**4**	**5**
Presents oral and written communication succinctly and with regard to its impact on the recipient.					
Presents self in a manner appropriate to the situation.					
Refers positively to the organisation, its people and its services.					
Presents relevant and well-reasoned arguments.					
Presents own point of view with conviction.					
Adapts and develops arguments to achieve results desired.					

behaviours are causing problems – and these may be different for each group of participants on the course.

Other information may be requested, such as previous training in a similar area, development activities already undertaken, and so on. However, remember that long and complex questionnaires have a lower return rate than short, straightforward ones.

Another source of information could be the results of a formal performance review. However, performance ratings are only a guide to current levels of competency – if competencies are being rated. Knowing that an individual has a low score against a sales objective will not help a trainer because that may be for a number of reasons. If, however, the organisation uses its competency framework to assess the 'how' of a job (as discussed in the performance review chapter – Chapter 4), then a low score in sales achievement coupled with a low score on influencing may give the trainer a more useful insight.

Performance review ratings may not be accurate measures of

competency alone because of their confidential nature and their link to pay reviews. Also, linking the results of 'what' ratings and 'how' ratings may lead to incorrect conclusions if other information is not available (such as the evidence behind the ratings). It is better, for training and development purposes, either to use another measure (eg the outcome of an assessment centre) or to supplement the rating with other information if performance review ratings are not reliable.

Skills audits are snapshots of the current competency levels in a particular business unit (from a team to the whole organisation). They are usually conducted with the primary objective of matching current competencies against those required in the future. A competency framework can assist in the collection of this information.

Depending on the number of people involved in the audit, the methods of collection might include:

❏ a review of training records
❏ questionnaires
❏ workshops
❏ interviews.

It is important for the purpose of the audit to be established before it is carried out in order to ensure that the correct amount of information is collected. For example, if a snapshot is required to get a feel for major areas of weakness in a company, a skills audit which interviewed every member of staff in the organisation would probably be unnecessary, unless the organisation was very small. Questionnaires, workshops and interviews with key individuals (eg samples of managers and job-holders) may be more appropriate.

A review of training records may highlight key areas of skills need by analysing the most popular events. However, unless training records include all types of event, this information will have to be supplemented with other data. Training records that just indicate the most popular courses and/or learning material will exclude the on-the-job training which occurs. Nor can such an analysis indicate if the popularity has peaked or the need has been met.

Questionnaires along the lines of the one shown in Table 22 can be used. They may be issued to:

❏ individuals to complete – considering their own skills or the skills of their colleagues in general
❏ line managers to complete – considering the skills of their teams.

Because the questionnaires will be focusing on perceived 'weaknesses' it is important to establish anonymity. This is vital even when asking managers to rate their staff. It is not inconceivable for managers to rate their team leniently, particularly if they feel the team lacks key skills and if they are the person responsible for training and development. The purpose of undertaking the questionnaire should be made clear and supported throughout the process. Promises of 'no blame' should not be broken by making people feel that the finger is being pointed at them for the results of the audit.

The results of a questionnaire can be explored further in interviews and/or workshops. Both methods can give useful insight into the reasons behind high or low scores on the audit. Because the purpose of interviews and workshops is to explore the reasons behind the results, the outputs should not be based on conjecture but should be the real experiences of the people being interviewed or on the workshop. For example, if a manager attends a workshop and puts forward the opinion that the reason for a low result on teamworking skills is a bad training course, then this opinion should be substantiated by factual evidence such as the results of evaluation exercises. If it cannot be substantiated, there is a danger that any plans based on the outcomes of the workshop or interviews may be misdirected.

Personal knowledge of the candidates may help a trainer prepare for the delivery of an event. This is most likely where the trainer is already part of a team (eg as the line manager). However, there is the obvious danger that assumptions can be made in place of exploring facts. The competency framework can, again, be a useful structure to explore areas of training and development need to help focus the learning and the teaching on to key behaviours. This could be done through the methods outlined above. For example: if a whole team is attending an event, a pre-event questionnaire could be used; if an individual is attending an event, an informal discussion could be structured around the competency framework.

Situations in which the learning could be put into practice

The best training and development events are those which relate not only to current skills but also to the actual situations in which the participant needs to use the skills. How many times have individuals sat in courses, seminars and so on and thought 'This is all very well, but it's not like this where I work'? It is not an easy task for a trainer to replicate the workplace exactly because it is rare that any two situations are exactly the same. However, the closer the link to 'reality' the better.

The right chemistry!

A staff satisfaction survey in a multinational oil and chemicals company revealed concerns regarding the way staff felt they were being managed. One option would have been to teach individuals how to manage through some form of standardised training programme. However, it would have been very difficult to account for the different circumstances in which people-management skills were required and the different levels of ability to be found in managers attending the programme.

It was decided to produce a development workshop which would provide supervisors and managers with an opportunity to be observed and get feedback while they managed people. Benchmarks for the workshop were five people-management competencies. Activities in the workshop were simulations of common situations in which people-management competencies would be found within the organisation – for example, appraisals and a meeting to communicate change to a team. Actors were used to play the team members of the supervisors and managers.

The workshop design ensured that each individual manager's people-management issues were identified and discussed in terms of further development. The programme, although common to all managers, was therefore able to address each individual manager's needs.

Although some managers and supervisors thought they would not gain from 'training in people management', all managers attending the workshop (over 200 supervisors and managers worldwide) praised its relevance and usefulness. The most cited reasons for this feedback were 'the realism of the simulations' and 'the quality of feedback from the actors and observers'.

A competency framework can help to ensure that training and development events are realistic. The more specific the framework, the closer the match to 'reality'. Behaviours drawn from situations encountered in the organisation, department, business unit, and so on, will reflect what is happening in that organisation. Those designing a training or development event will then have ready-made guidance in the design of simulation exercises.

To illustrate this point we refer back to our **Appendix Framework**. A training workshop designed to help managers set objectives for their staff will relate closely to the 'ACHIEVING RESULTS: Objective-setting' competency. From the behaviours outlined in this competency (assuming we are aiming at 'level 2') we know that any simulation exercises have to ensure that the managers get the opportunity to:

❑ identify and set clear objectives
❑ establish success and measurement criteria
❑ enrol the support of others for achieving objectives
❑ review and adapt objectives to meet changing needs.

We may also include Level 1 behaviours:

❑ ensure that objectives are achievable within already agreed commitments
❑ agree appropriate success and measurement criteria
❑ identify and highlight potential obstacles in achieving objectives.

Exercises with these behaviours in mind will relate to reality because these behaviours come from reality.

It is important, however, not to rely totally on the competency framework for context information. Each team will be facing different scenarios, and training and development events will be enhanced with such details as the current situation in a team, upcoming changes (procedurally or within the structure of the organisation), and so on.

It is worth mentioning development centres here. We feel there is an important distinction between centres that are designed to assess an individual's competency against a predetermined benchmark, and centres which give an individual the opportunity to practise techniques – eg our example, **The right chemistry**. The first type of centre is an assessment process in which marks are often allocated and action plans for future development are often directed at a specific future role. Such assessment-for-development centres (ADCs) are effectively the same as assessment centres for selection with the possible exceptions of the extent of feedback – which is more wide-ranging – and the outcome – no participant is actually selected at that stage. ADCs are covered in the chapter on reviewing performance (Chapter 4).

The second type of centre has a purely developmental focus. It is a realistic work simulation in which the participant's behaviour is observed. Performance is not rated; rather, participants are encouraged to reflect on what they did and compare this with what is expected. Learning points and action plans from such development centres are directed to further development within each individual's current role, or one for which he or she has already been selected.

Both types of centre may use similar activities but the purposes, the outcomes and the processes are different.

Available training expertise

Not all trainers are able to deliver all training events. Not all managers are skilful enough to support all development activities. Competencies could be linked to a system which identifies who can do what in the way of delivery and/or support. For example, training events which involve dealing with senior managers may require a higher level of 'influencing' than events with more junior staff. Also, development activities which involve a mentoring relationship may require a higher level of 'managing relationships' than those which involve more straightforward support.

This method of categorising competencies needed for particular events or activities may work well for a training department, which may be linking competency to progression anyway. However, it is likely to be a much more complex task across a whole organisation.

The selection of an appropriate training and development event or activity

Once a training and/or development need has been identified, an appropriate way of meeting that need has to be found. Training needs are more likely to be met through formal training events; development needs through informal development activities. There are several ways in which suitable events are made public (eg directories of training courses) but development activities are often less well communicated.

Competency frameworks can be used to identify suitable activities by matching events and activities against each competency level and even against behavioural indicators. These can be reproduced in a directory available to everyone in the organisation. Table 23 is an example page of a fictional directory based on our sample competency framework.

Competency frameworks can help to develop these sorts of directories because the behavioural indicators guide what activities belong where. In Table 23 there is mention of a video called *On Being a Team Member*. This perhaps does not, at

---

'Plugging' into the system

A paper-based development directory was produced for a life assurance company. It was very popular with sales staff, for whom it was designed, and other staff wanted something similar. This resulted in a number of directories, each of which required reprinting and redistribution when adapted and/or updated.

Many of the activities in the different directories were similar, and of course core competencies were present in each directory. So a single directory was produced which covered all jobs. This single directory took existing directories and 'plugged' them straight into a specially-developed computer package. Updating and distribution is now much easier.

The computer package also provides much greater flexibility because it can in turn have any new directories 'plugged' into it and can be linked to computer-based performance reviews. This enables reviewers to go through the full process of collecting and reviewing behavioural feedback and then establishing development events and activities to address development needs.

first glance, seem to fit with a development need for 'planning'. However, one of the behaviours in Planning, Level 1, is 'Avoids negative impact of own actions on others'. The second section of this video may help to highlight the impact of not planning one's daily tasks properly on the members of one's team.

Drawing up such a directory is clearly a time-consuming task if it is to be comprehensive. It also requires constant maintenance to ensure that it remains valid. However, many companies now use technology for drafting, and even communicating, training and development directories, which makes life easier for all concerned.

Table 23
EXAMPLE OF EVENTS AND ACTIVITIES TO MEET TRAINING AND DEVELOPMENT NEED(S)

ACHIEVING RESULTS: Planning		
Level 1: Prioritises day-to-day workload		
Suggested training events:		
How to make use of a diary	workshop	1/2 day on site
Time management	course	2 days off site
How to prioritise	distance learning course (video and workbook)	estimated 5 hours
Priorities, Priorities	video	1 1/2 hours
Suggested development events and activities:		
Note: You may find it helpful to undertake these activities with the knowledge and support of your line manager. Set timescales for reviewing progress. Discuss the outcomes with your line manager and agree follow-up actions if needed. ❑ Use a diary or time-planner to schedule future plans. ❑ Use a 'To Do' list for daily tasks. ❑ Watch Section 2 of the video *On Being a Team Member* (takes about 1 hour). Consider the impact of your actions on others, and think of any appropriate action you can take to minimise the possibility of negative impact on others resulting from your actions. ❑ Make estimates at the start of each day of how far through your work you think you will be at certain times (eg mid-morning, lunch, mid-afternoon). Compare this with your actual progress, and reflect on any differences. ❑ Make a list of what you view as your key tasks. Check this against your job description or objectives, or with your line manager, to check that they agree.		

Exactly which event or activity to choose will depend on the environmental and individual factors that influence training and development mentioned at the beginning of the chapter.

The evaluation of training and development events and activities

The successful outcome of any training event should be

- ❏ in the short term that the individuals learned the techniques they were supposed to learn (ie the event achieved its objectives)
- ❏ in the longer term that the individuals successfully put the techniques into practice through undergoing development activities (ie the individuals achieve their objectives).

Over time these should ensure that the organisation achieves its own training objectives.

Evaluating the success of training and development has caused organisations many headaches. Not least, it is difficult to know whether any improvement in skills is down to the training event or to circumstances that would have happened anyway – particularly when measuring across a large number of people. For example, was last month's increase in profits a result of the customer services training or of the article in a daily newspaper that showed our product as one of the best?

While it is common sense for organisations to ensure that they are not wasting money on training and development, the financial evaluation of such events and activities are beyond the scope of this book. However, measuring whether learning objectives have been met, and therefore the worth of the event or activity in terms of time and effort, can be achieved using competency frameworks.

Assessing how successful an event has been in achieving its objectives is reasonably straightforward – provided that the event had clear objectives, of course. Traditionally, this sort of evaluation has been effected through a questionnaire given out at the end of an event. These questionnaires explore many different factors of the event, such as:

- ❏ the materials used
- ❏ the delivery of the material
- ❏ opportunities to ask questions

- ❏ the quality of the answers to questions
- ❏ relevance to own situation
- ❏ the pace of the event
- ❏ whether the stated objectives were met.

This sort of information can also be collected orally – although there are issues of confidentiality, especially if the trainer is the one who is collecting the information. Even the most assertive person may find it hard to give negative feedback about an event to the person who ran it.

Although this sort of evaluation may yield useful information about the event itself, it is a mistake to translate this to the success (or otherwise) of the learning. In other words, getting good feedback on a course does not necessarily mean that all the participants are now experts. To refer back to our driving-test analogy at the beginning of this chapter, a series of excellent driving lessons which the learner enjoyed does not necessarily mean that he or she will become a skilful driver.

The more relevant sort of evaluation when it comes to assessing the worth of time and effort is that of the success of learners in achieving their objectives. This, as with the evaluation of events, assumes that objectives have been agreed.

Learning objectives of an individual

The learning objectives of an individual are essentially the same as any other performance objective. What is it that the individual wants or needs to achieve, and how is he or she going to do it? There will often also be a development action plan agreed which covers the support the individual will receive back in the job to transfer the learning to the workplace. The learning objectives should be agreed between the individual and the line manager before any training or development takes place. Ideally, no event should even be arranged until the learning objectives have been agreed.

The competency framework can assist in drawing up these objectives. The behavioural indicators will help the individual and the line manager focus on what should change when learning has successfully taken place. For example, if an individual has a need to learn some creative thinking techniques (for 'DEVELOPING THE BUSINESS: Generating and building on ideas, Level 2' of our **Appendix Framework**), the learning objectives will include one or more of the behaviours of Level 2. Table 24 shows an example of learning objectives and an action plan in this case.

At an appropriate time after the event, these objectives should be assessed. By focusing on behaviours not only is the learning of the techniques questioned (eg did Chris learn three approaches to creative thinking?) but also whether the techniques are making the required difference (ie has Chris's behaviour changed?).

Deciding who should collect such evaluation information is an important consideration. At line manager or department level, 'global' information is lost. At a central point, 'local' information is lost. A better system would be to ensure that managers are responsible for the collection of the information (after all, they are the ones who are in the best position to feed back the success of the learning) and that a central point (usually the training department) is responsible for the collation of the results. This way, not only can the managers keep a track of the investment of time and effort of themselves and

Table 24

EXAMPLE OF LEARNING OBJECTIVES AND ACTION PLAN

Learning objectives for Chris Smith – Creative Thinking techniques

What
❏   To learn three different approaches to creative thinking.
❏   To learn a process for assessing the feasibility of ideas.
❏   To learn the company's procedure for putting ideas forward for acceptance.

How
❏   To develop new processes or practices to accommodate new ideas.
❏   To assess feasibility of ideas for the business.
❏   To promote leading ideas with energy and enthusiasm.

Action plan
❏   Attend Creative Thinking techniques workshop.
❏   Attend the marketing department's 'New ideas' forum once a week.
❏   Contribute at least three new ideas to the forum by the end of May.
❏   Get at least one idea passed by the forum.
❏   Meet with line manager once a fortnight for support and to discuss progress.

their team members but the organisation can ensure that training and development events are achieving the learning that the strategy requires.

Of course, low results from such evaluation may not mean that the event was poor – it may mean that there is another training need or that the action plan was not adhered to. With detailed objectives using behavioural statements, such as those illustrated in Table 24, it can be decided not only whether the effort of the event was worth while (ie did Chris meet the objectives?) but also why there was any shortfall.

Collation of evaluation data can produce useful information about how closely a business unit is meeting its strategic plans. For example, an organisation introduces a culture change programme with a particular focus on teamwork. This organisation would expect to see training and development events designed around 'teamworking' competencies to be having the desired effect. Investigation of reasons for any shortfall may highlight areas that need attention either in support terms or in further training and development needs.

Setting standards for progress

There are three main forms of monitoring the progress of an individual:

❑ within a job (eg an apprenticeship)
❑ within an organisation (eg a management training scheme)
❑ within a profession (eg through the various levels of accountancy)

Progress has traditionally been monitored largely through serving time and passing various exams or tests. These are reasonably straightforward criteria to measure and obviously have some bearing on the expertise of an individual. However, the system does miss out on the measurement of behaviour, and this is where competencies can help.

Progress within a job

This sort of monitoring is where progress towards a specific goal is measured. The goal is the successful achievement of a level of competence required to carry out a job successfully.

There is usually an expectation that the goal will be achieved within a certain time frame. Although there may be 'promotion' and/or salary increases attached to the successful achievement of certain stages of the process, progress is usually within one particular job.

Grades within grades

A mortgage company introduced a competency-based training and development programme for its multi-functional clerical staff (let us call them 'C'-grade staff). To progress from a new starter (C1) to a fully competent member of staff (C3) could take up to two years. The programme was designed around three key modules. The first was introductory and had to be completed first. The next two modules could be completed in either order.

On successful completion of the introductory module plus one other the individual was promoted from C1 to C2 and given a pay rise. On successful completion of the third module, the individual was promoted to C3, again with a pay rise. This promotion and salary increase was not only motivational for the staff member but it also differentiated between the various levels of skill within a grade and recognised achievement.

The attainment of skill must include the training of the necessary techniques as well as development events and activities. This is likely to take the form of a mix of different training methods over a period of time and may well be prescribed regardless of the individual – ie all trainees go through the same programme. Competencies can assist not only in the structure of the training programme by giving a focus to its objectives (as discussed earlier in the section on the design of training and development events) but also in the later structure of the development that happens 'on-the-job'.

Behavioural indicators can be used to structure a development programme, but a decision needs to be made first about which competencies will be measured during progress. These are likely to be the ones perceived as being important for the successful completion of a job. If competencies are listed in job descriptions or job profiles, then it clearly makes sense to use them because the work has already been done in identifying the competencies required.

If role profiles have not been established, one way of identifying critical competencies or competency levels is to use a process similar to that used for identifying recruitment-critical competencies. For example:

1   List the most critical job tasks required to meet the job purpose.
2   List the competencies (or competency levels) that would be required to undertake each of these tasks.
3   Rank these competencies (levels) in order of their importance to completing the tasks.

Another approach that can be very effective is called 'paired comparisons'. This approach provides a more accurate assessment of importance. Following this approach, competencies are scored according to their relevance to each key task or activity. To do this, each competency is compared in turn with every other competency, identifying which is the more important in each pairing to achieving the task or activity. In this way, scores for the importance of each of the competencies to each task or activity can be produced. There is insufficient space here to describe the approach fully, but a brief example is provided in **Appendix 2** and many books on problem-solving techniques describe this technique in detail.

These steps can be undertaken with existing job-holders and/or their managers because these individuals should have the most realistic view of the job. In many cases it is likely that job-critical competencies will have been identified during the production of the competency framework, or later if selection against competencies was used to fill job/role vacancies.

It is easier to use behavioural indicators that have been adapted specifically to the job in which the individual is being developed. This not only makes it easier for the individual to understand the relevance of the measures but also makes it easier for the person who is designing and assessing the development activities to be clear about the objectives of the programme. If using a generic framework, behavioural indicators will have to be adapted. Advice on how to do this is covered in the chapter on producing a competency framework (Chapter 2).

When using behavioural indicators for the measurement of

progress, there will be some additional information gained which may be useful – either within the customisation process or additional to it. This includes such details as:

- the context in which the behaviours are to be demonstrated (for example, what exactly is the definition of 'organisation' in the behaviour 'Builds own knowledge of the organisation, its people and its services'?)
- the limits which behaviours are not expected to exceed (for example, what decisions would not be included in the behaviour 'Obtains and uses necessary information to make decisions'?)
- the underlying knowledge that is required (for example, what would individuals need to know about before they could develop skills that demonstrate their competence in 'Gathers and maintains information'?).

Once a competency profile for the job has been agreed, the training and development programme should aim to ensure that individuals have the necessary techniques and development opportunities to demonstrate the required behaviours. This means that development activities must allow the techniques learned to be practised in a variety of appropriate situations. Activities are therefore likely to include a range of methods such as on-the-job coaching and simulations.

Factors that need to be considered when deciding on how progress is going to be measured include:

- What will be assessed? Will there be an assessment of knowledge, behaviour, skills, or a combination of some or all of these?
- How will skills, knowledge and behaviour be assessed? For example, skills and behaviour can be displayed only during the execution of a task or activity.
- How will objectivity be ensured?
- When will an individual be 'assessed'? Will this be at set times or when a certain level of skill is seen to have been achieved?
- Who will assess performance? Will it be the line manager, someone external to the team, or someone external to the company?

❏ How will consistency of assessment be assured?
❏ What will be the result of successful completion of each stage? Will there be a pay or grade increase?
❏ What will be the result of unsuccessful completion of a stage? Will there be remedial training and development? How many times can an individual re-do a particular stage? How long can an individual be on the programme overall?

A competency framework can assist in many of these factors, in particular in the factors that affect the measurement process – ie those covered in the first three bullet-points of the above list.

Having used competencies to state what is required in the training and development programme, measurement should obviously match these objectives. Setting learning objectives is covered earlier in this chapter. However, guidelines on how to measure learning objectives on programmes of progression must be made clear to ensure consistency. These guidelines would cover such issues as:

❏ what evidence is acceptable (eg copies of written work produced, random checks on telephone calls with customers)
❏ how many times an individual must demonstrate a behaviour before being deemed to have 'passed'
❏ how evidence can be produced where opportunities to demonstrate a particular behaviour are infrequent.

These guidelines must be available to the participants in the programme as well as to the assessors. It is advisable that how an individual is to be assessed is made clear. Even in situations where there are to be spot checks it should be made clear that these will happen over a specified period of time. Without such openness there is a danger that the programme becomes seen as a 'spying' process, and that suspicions are aroused about the true purpose of the assessment.

Although success on the training and development programme should be the key aim of everyone involved, it should be made clear to participants what the results of failure will be. For example, if a trainee's continued employment depends on successful completion of the programme, it should be made clear at the outset.

Assessment of individual progress, particularly in job- or salary-rise-dependent programmes, must be objective and fair. This is not only so that the organisation focuses its efforts correctly but also to avoid accusations of unfair treatment – eg because of the team people work in or the manager they work for. Using a competency framework, especially one that has already been established, as the benchmark against which progress is measured is a good way of achieving objectivity.

NVQ/SVQs are based on the measurement of competence (ie output or task). Organisations may use this sort of framework to monitor progress within a job. If a competency framework exists within the organisation, careful attention should be paid to how the competencies link to the NVQ/SVQ. A key question is how an individual's behaviours are going to be measured alongside his or her achievement of output-based objectives.

Progress within an organisation

This sort of monitoring is usually focused on the progress of an individual to a level within an organisation rather than within a specific job. This is typical of progression through a management training scheme when the final job that an individual will undertake is not known at the outset of the programme. This is also typical of the product of succession-planning by which the skills of a population are to be improved or increased without anyone's necessarily knowing when those skills will be used, or in what part of the organisation. Time-frames for 'success' are usually fairly flexible, where they exist at all, and learning objectives tend to be more generic.

Measuring progress in management-training-type schemes may often be overlaid with progress within a particular job. For example, if the programme involves stints of a particular length of time in various departments, the trainee may well have specific learning objectives during each stint as well as learning objectives within the management training programme itself. It is important that there is clarity about who is supporting and measuring what objectives. Without this clarity there is a danger that the management trainee becomes an 'odd-job' member of the team – ie the person who does the things that no one else wants to do and who learns little other than how to make coffee and use the photocopier!

Measuring development progress within a programme designed to address succession-planning issues will vary depending on how the need was identified and what the solution is that has been put in place to address it. For example, if the need was identified through assessment-for-development centres, the measurement is likely to be focused on the learning objectives of those individuals who have been through the centre. If the need was identified through a general awareness of lack of necessary successors (eg as a result of unsuccessful internal recruitment campaigns), measurement may simply be against the evaluation of training events and development activities, performance reviews and/or analysis of future recruitment campaigns. However, the programmes that are most successful when addressing succession-planning issues are the ones that have clear objectives which result in a focused approach to address them. Hoping that people will develop when there is no clear process for them to undertake such development is perhaps taking too optimistic an approach to the problem.

The factors mentioned in the previous section regarding measurement of progress all apply here too. Again, competencies can help in similar ways. However, in this process there are differences. As mentioned above, learning objectives may be more generic – that is, they may concentrate more on 'management' competencies which have been identified as core throughout the business at a particular level rather than on competencies specific to a particular job role.

If a competency framework has been designed for a whole organisation (as opposed to only one part of it), the behavioural indicators will already be in a generic form. They can therefore be easily established within a development programme as standards to achieve and as indicators of success. For example, a management trainee programme is likely to include generic management competencies which apply to whatever position the trainee holds at any one point in his or her programme.

Some work will have to be done to ensure that a clear process of measuring such behaviours is in place. The bullet-points mentioned above covering the guidelines on measuring performance against learning objectives all apply here too.

However, there should also be consideration of whether there is movement between levels within a competency. For example, during the trainees' time on a management training scheme, are they expected to progress from Level 1 to Level 2 (or further) in some competencies? If so, how will this progress be assessed?

Succession-planning and management training schemes both have dual learning objectives. There are the ones for the job being done at a particular time, and there are the ones for the level that the individual is aspiring to. Care should be taken when designing development activities to ensure that the required behaviours of the future competencies are practised. The competency framework can only provide a focus for such activities, and many other factors – not least the willingness of the individual and his or her manager to support such development – play an important part in the optimal results of succession or management training programmes.

Progress within a profession

More often than not, measurement of progress within a profession is conducted and/or controlled by bodies outside the organisation in which the individual is employed. Progress is also likely to be measured against a framework which is established by a professional body and which applies nationally. This means that progress is often measured via the results of examinations and tests. Competency frameworks may well play a part in the criteria for success, but there is usually a heavy emphasis on knowledge rather than behaviour.

Once an individual is a member of a profession (and this would include student membership), it is not unusual for that profession to expect certain behaviours from that member. These expectations are often enshrined in codes of practice. In some professions it would be possible to be struck off the register of acknowledged professionals if these codes of practice were not adhered to.

Within an organisation there may well be other success criteria that an individual would have to meet to move through the internal hierarchy within a profession. For example, obtaining corporate membership of the Institute of Personnel and Development may be a requirement before an individual is promoted to a certain level, but achievement of the membership may not, alone, be enough to result in automatic promotion.

If an organisation is going to add other requirements for progression within a profession to suit internal needs, it is important that both sets of learning objectives are matched. For learning objectives not to match could lead to conflicts between what the organisation demands and what the professional body demands. If the organisation supports an external programme, it should be addressing any such conflicts before they become issues for the learner. This is particularly important when considering the competencies that may be overlaid on such a development programme. It is not unusual for the culture within a company to demand behaviour from an individual contrary to that which is expected from the professional body to which they belong. For example, pressure may be put on personnel managers to recruit people into the organisation in a way which would contravene best practice as proposed by the Institute of Personnel and Development.

While such situations may be a matter for the professional to deal with, it is worth considering these potential conflicts. How will a development programme that contains learning objectives built around behaviours which contradict a professional code of conduct be managed by the organisation?

Apart from this issue, the setting of learning objectives and the measurement of progress against these objectives is very similar to the first section about measuring progress within a job.

In brief

Two key purposes for training and development activity are to ensure that the competencies of staff are sufficient to meet both current and future needs. A wide range of factors influence not only what training and development events and activities are offered by an organisation but also how much actual learning takes place. Organisational strategic plans and policies will affect what training and development is on offer. Environmental factors, especially the culture of the organisation, and individual factors such as learning style, motivation and abilities, will affect how much individuals actually learn.

Training is about the teaching of techniques. Development is about the practice of those techniques in a focused and supported manner, resulting in skill and expertise. Ways to achieve this result are many and varied, but both parts of the equation must be in place to ensure success. Training events that are not followed up with development activities result in the techniques learned soon being forgotten. Development activities undertaken in ignorance of the necessary techniques required for success will result in errors. Both will cause frustration and lack of progress towards the individual's and the organisation's longer-term plans.

Competency frameworks can assist in many of the key stages of training and development – from identifying the need to designing the event and measuring not only the success of the event but the progress of individuals through structured programmes. However, competencies on their own will not make a success of any one stage. The use of a competency framework helps to focus each stage, but without skilled people to design, deliver and support the events and activities, competency-based training and development will be no better than any other poorly-resourced process.

6 USING COMPETENCIES TO SUPPORT PAY AND GRADING

In this chapter 'pay' refers to the financial rewards individuals receive for their work; 'grading' refers to structures which distinguish between jobs on the basis of perceived value to the business.

We have combined pay and grading in this chapter because of the frequency with which they are linked together when competencies are discussed in relation to either. However, the linking of these two topics can create confusion because although a competency-based pay system may be usefully linked to a competency-based grading system (and vice versa), it is not essential to have both. We will try to make clear distinctions between both aspects to avoid such confusion.

The purpose of pay and grading

Grading is about the perceived value which a job adds to the organisation. Pay is the financial reward somebody receives for doing a job, and is nearly always linked to the performance of job-holders. Even in companies where there is no formal performance-related pay system it is likely that there will be some link between pay and performance – people won't be paid for doing a bad job for very long.

Pay and grading are most often linked when job grades set limits for the rewards available to a job-holder. The job-holder's job performance then determines what pay he or she will receive within the grade limits. If only it was that simple in practice!

Grading structures usually represent differences in the perceived value of levels of responsibility and other job characteristics which make up jobs in an organisation. The reward structure is overlaid on the grading structure, indicating the range of reward for ranges of job grades. The job grading structure is thus the basic rationale for the distribution of the pay budget. This is a somewhat crude summary – but it captures what happens in most organisations.

From the job-holder's viewpoint the reward structures within a job grade represent earning potential, and job performance represents current reward. Where competencies are included in performance reviews and job grading, the expectation should therefore be that ratings of competency will have a direct influence on an individual's earnings. Where there is a direct link between competency ratings and the financial reward an individual receives, we would normally call this 'competency-based pay'.

We said earlier that pay is the reward for doing a job, but that a pay structure may have many and varied purposes. However, the key purposes would include:

❑ motivation
❑ rewarding performance fairly
❑ the retention and attraction of staff
❑ recognition of achievement
❑ confirmation and support of the organisation's culture.

Likewise, the purposes of a grading structure will vary between organisations, but are likely to include:

❑ setting pay bands – within market rates or not
❑ assisting in management of the pay budget
❑ recognition of value/job worth – internally
❑ recognition of value/job worth – externally
❑ providing motivation for development
❑ providing a structure for succession.

A pay structure, when linked to a grading structure, may well have overlapping minimum and maximum levels – that is, the maximum salary of one grade may be more than the minimum salary of the next grade. This allows for the means of recognising that experienced people, performing to a high standard, are more valuable to an organisation, at least in the short term, than a trainee on the next grade. Organisations may also decide to fix a point around which an individual who is able to do the job, and does so to an acceptable level of performance, is paid. Above this point are paid high-performers and more experienced individuals; below this point are paid low-performers or trainees.

Colourful rewards

A major finance company subdivides its job grades into colour zones. In each job grade there is a blue zone based on the level of competency expected of a trainee. The next colour zone is amber, which indicates the level of competency for minimum effective performance within the job. Finally, there is a red zone which describes the level of competency which would be observed of individuals contributing above the minimum effective level.

The pay bands for job grades are divided into these three zones. Individuals, therefore know the range of pay they are likely to receive depending on their level of competency. In addition, the zones provide some indication of, and motivation for, development of competencies required in the job.

Figure 4 shows how this type of pay and grading system might look. It is not unusual for this sort of system to have wider and more overlapping bands for more senior grades. There is often a wider range of jobs that fit into these grades with the requirement for a wide range of salaries.

Whatever grading system is used, in order that jobs can be positioned in it some form of evaluation mechanism is employed. There are many evaluation systems, ranging from those which are complex and analyse many features of a job, to the more simple, which focus on the relative worth of a whole job. They are all attempts at identifying the worth of a job to an organisation in order that the individual who holds that job can be remunerated correctly. The factors governing what 'correct' remuneration means will vary between sectors, professions and organisations, and even within organisations.

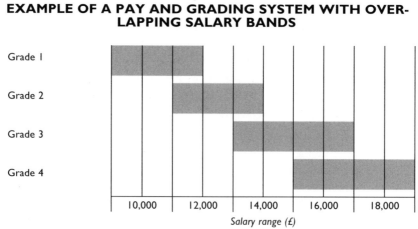

Figure 4

EXAMPLE OF A PAY AND GRADING SYSTEM WITH OVER-LAPPING SALARY BANDS

Salary range (£)

Factors influencing pay and grading

The factors that influence the pay policy and structure in an organisation vary depending on what system that organisation has put in place. However, all structures are likely to include such considerations as:

❑ the contribution of the individual
❑ the value of the individual to the organisation
❑ the scarcity of potential job-holders
❑ time served in the company and/or job
❑ the cost of living
❑ the financial position of the organisation
❑ other benefits/bonuses/incentives making up an overall remuneration package
❑ the frequency of pay reviews
❑ how quickly changes may be needed to respond to market pressures
❑ the success (or otherwise) of the organisation
❑ agreements with unions, staff associations, etc
❑ legal restrictions.

The factors that influence the grading policy and structure are likely to include:

❑ the contribution to the organisation of work outputs
❑ the organisational structure
❑ the organisation's size
❑ external benchmarking
❑ the job evaluation system/policy.

Combining these factors, when considering an integrated pay and grading structure, shows that the area is a complex one.

The contribution of competencies to pay and grading

As mentioned above, when pay and grading structures are linked there has to be some way of identifying

❑ which grade a certain job belongs to
❑ how much pay, within a set band, an individual should receive for the job he or she does.

We will look at each of these factors separately.

Grading structures

Although some job evaluation systems have included competency-like factors, such as 'decision-making', very few incorporate competency frameworks directly into their equations for establishing the relative worth of a job. Where competencies have been brought into pay and grading, the most common application appears to be in setting pay bands. This is not competency-based job evaluation, for the grade structure produced by the original evaluation system is usually left intact.

Most job evaluation systems fall into one of three categories:

❑ *individual negotiation* – where each job-holder is 'graded' on his or her specific skills, abilities, etc. In effect this is unlikely to result in grades as such because it is the person who holds the job that is evaluated as much as the job itself. This sort of system is typical of the professional sports and entertainment industries.
❑ *whole-job ranking* – comparing the value of a job within an organisation with the value of other jobs. This approach is

not analytical in that the detail or component parts of a job are not analysed separately; instead, the job is considered as a whole.

❑ *factor comparisons* – where component parts of a job are analysed and 'marks' are given in relation to the relative worth of that factor. Marks are added up and an overall score for the job is calculated.

Each of these systems requires a valuation of what is important to the organisation – ie the features of a job that make it worth more, or less, than other jobs. In the past these features have often been the size of the budget, the complexity of the decisions being made by the job-holder, the number of staff being managed, the knowledge required to undertake the job, and so on. In fact, most of the features are outputs – ie the result of tasks: the 'what' of the job. Some organisations are now introducing inputs, the 'how' of the job, into job evaluation and grading, and this is where competencies start to feature.

In an integrated competency approach it makes sense to include the factors that are considered key in recruitment, training, development and performance management into the job evaluation and grading systems. This is not a straightforward process because grading is about jobs rather than performance. However, the key way in which competency frameworks can assist in the grading process is by adding an extra element to the question 'What is valued in this organisation – ie what features make one job worth more, or less, than another?'

When jobs are being analysed for evaluation purposes, it is to investigate the features already deemed important to an organisation. If a competency framework exists for that organisation, it is not unreasonable for the level of competency required to do that job to be taken into account. However, there does seem to be a need for some caution to be exercised. Although many competency frameworks are split into levels, this is rarely done solely on the basis of job grade. So although there may be a relationship between the job level within the organisation and the competency level required to undertake that job, it is not always so.

We warned against the use of grades to indicate competency levels in the chapter **What do we mean by competencies?** (Chapter 1). The same, in reverse, can be said in this section. It is unlikely to be appropriate to use competency levels to set grading structures. This is because the competency framework is designed to show different levels, within each competency, of behaviour. Some competencies may have a different number of levels from another. The same job may require a different level of each competency.

Figure 5 illustrates the different levels of competency in a generic framework with nine competencies (not the **Appendix Framework** used in this book). It would be difficult to tie the levels of this framework to grades because not all competencies consist of the same number of levels. So, for example, it would not be possible to say that all senior management jobs were at Level 4 because only two competencies go up to that level.

Figures 6 and 7 show two job profiles overlaid on the generic framework. The first is a junior job, the second a more senior one. The shaded areas indicate the competency levels required.

In neither of the two examples do the jobs require all competencies at the same level. We can also see that the job in Example 2 (Figure 7) actually requires a 'lower' level of competency 5 than the more junior job. To tie competency levels

Figure 5
GRAPHIC PRESENTATION OF COMPETENCY LEVELS IN A CORE FRAMEWORK

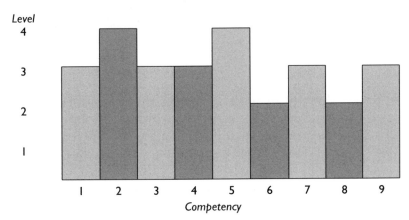

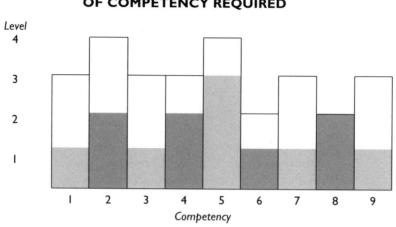

Figure 6

**EXAMPLE 1: JOB PROFILE SHOWING DIFFERENT LEVELS
OF COMPETENCY REQUIRED**

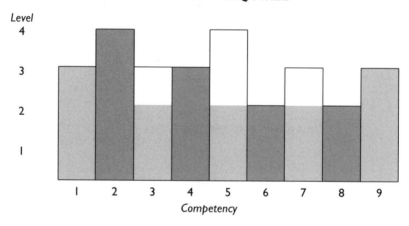

Figure 7

**EXAMPLE 2: JOB PROFILE SHOWING DIFFERENT LEVELS
OF COMPETENCY REQUIRED**

directly in with grades in these circumstances would require extensive manipulation of either the competency framework or the grading system. Neither option is really workable.

A better use of competency frameworks is to balance competency levels with other features – for example, by allocating 'marks' to the various competencies and levels and including the overall results with the scores obtained by rating other features. This may seem reasonably straightforward, but it raises a number of such issues as:

❏ How many 'marks' would the different levels be awarded?
❏ Are all competencies to be rated as equal – or are some more valuable than others and therefore worthy of a weighting?
❏ Could the same competency/level be valued differently in different jobs?
❏ Where are the benchmarks for comparison going to come from?

Obtaining the answers to these questions will involve a lot of data-gathering and analysis. However, once completed, a comprehensive, tailored job evaluation system will be possible.

An alternative, interim approach being taken by some organisations is to overlay the competency profiles for each job on the grading system. This is then used to link the results from assessment processes (including performance reviews) with the level of pay an individual should receive. The decision regarding where to position the pay of an individual in this case is linked to the achievement of certain levels of competency. For example, the job may require a competency at Level 2. Job-holders who have not reached that level of competency may be paid differently from those who have.

Once competency requirements become a feature of job evaluation systems, competency frameworks could help in the collection of data. This can be by providing a structure to elicit information about the requirements of each job. If the jobs being investigated already have competency profiles, the behaviours of the competencies can be used to structure questionnaires or interviews. For example, a job requiring Level 2 from the 'ACHIEVING RESULTS: Planning' competency in our **Appendix Framework**, might result in questions to job-holders that included:

❏ How would someone in this job estimate resources to achieve plans?
❏ What plans would someone in this job have to work to?
❏ How would someone in this job build alternative actions into plans to deal with likely contingencies?

❑ How would someone in this job communicate plans?

❑ Who are the relevant people to whom such plans would have to be communicated?

Such questions would have to be phrased carefully in order to ensure that information is being gathered about the job, and not necessarily about the person in that job. The information that is gathered from such questions could then be included with other data gathered for the evaluation process being used by the organisation.

Once jobs are evaluated, they have to be matched against an agreed grading system. The grading systems that organisations use vary enormously. Grading systems can be based on

❑ straightforward hierarchies – eg grades 1–10, with 1 the most junior and 10 the most senior

❑ various types of job – eg management, technical, clerical, executive

❑ levels within grades – eg four different levels within each grade, so a job might be Grade 1 but there might be a trainee, application, expert and coach level

❑ roles – eg researchers, consultants, senior consultants and partners in a professional organisation.

Organisations may have a number of different grading systems in place to take account of different needs within different parts of the business.

Once a grading system has been agreed, it is usual for it to be used to set pay. As with the grading system itself, there are various methods for setting pay against grading. These include systems where basic pay is

❑ set very precisely against each level/grade – ie every person on the same level/grade will earn the same basic pay

❑ set as a range between minimum and maximum – ie people on the same level/grade could be on different salaries, but not less than the minimum, or more than the maximum

❑ not set to any limits – ie negotiated with the individual based on what they can bring to the organisation.

The level of pay agreed against the grading system is likely to change from time to time. Many organisations regularly negotiate new pay levels (usually each year). The grading system is, however, unlikely to change unless there is organisational change.

Once a grading system has been agreed and pay levels matched against it, the performance of the individuals who hold jobs in the organisation needs to be assessed. The outcome of these assessments will then contribute to the decisions made about levels of pay an individual will receive.

Pay

There are various component parts to 'pay'. These include:

❑ basic pay
❑ commission
❑ bonuses
❑ profit-sharing
❑ allowances.

Many of these will be linked either to length of service (eg some bonuses will be awarded only to individuals who have been employed for a certain length of time, regardless of their grade) or directly to the grade or role an individual holds (eg some allowances will be payable only to people in certain job grades). Other elements of pay, however, are often linked to the performance of an individual (eg basic pay in performance-related pay schemes or commission). Competency frameworks can contribute where pay is linked to performance.

The main advantage of using competencies to set pay bands is that this should help to:

❑ link job performance to reward
❑ make job value appear more open
❑ demonstrate a developmental progression for reward.

Linking job performance to reward

There have been many debates about the relevance of linking performance with pay in a direct way. A key point in these debates is whether pay should be to reward people for past performance or to motivate them to perform well in the future, or both. A position that causes less heated debate is that lack of money (as perceived by the job-holder) in relation to input of effort and the type of job being undertaken is perceived to be demotivating. This book takes no position in this debate – but for the purposes of this chapter we will assume that performance does have a bearing on pay, and that organisations who make this link will want to make it as objective as possible.

Most performance-related pay (PRP) systems require performance to be measured against objectives or targets of some sort, and the outcome of the assessment to be linked to the pay increase that the individual will receive. The subject of measuring performance has already been covered in depth elsewhere in this book (primarily Chapter 4). This section looks at how the outcomes of that measurement can be tied in to pay.

The outcomes of performance review and assessment are likely to be in the form of one or more ratings. This may be based on outputs (ie what has been achieved) or inputs (ie how it has been achieved), or a combination of both. In many pay systems that measure inputs as well as outputs the final rating is a single digit or letter which is arrived at by combining ratings given for both elements.

Whatever rating approach is used there should be some link between the rating (ie the performance of an individual) and the resulting pay decision. Whether pay is seen as a motivator and/or a reward, everyone in the organisation needs to be sure how their performance assessments link in with their pay awards.

The link between performance assessments and pay awards must also tie in with pay and grading policy. For example, if the policy states that the highest pay awards are to go to those with the highest performance scores, this must be seen to be happening. That, of course, assumes that the pay and grading policy is correct and fair, and is properly implemented too. Discrepancies between the results of performance-related pay awards and the pay policy may be a sign that the policy needs review!

In communicating the pay and grading policy, the competency framework – if it is relevant – should be referred to. As with grading, using competencies to link performance with pay will reinforce the framework's relevance across all the aspects of managing people. This also reinforces the importance which the organisation gives to behaviour in performance. If the people in an organisation have access to the framework, there should be no secrets over how their performance links with their pay when it comes to competencies.

Mixed messages

An international electronics consumer goods company introduced a competency-based development programme. However, the majority of its staff received pay increases and bonuses based primarily upon targets for the sales of products.

Although some work was under way to link competencies to the pay and grading system, nothing had been done to communicate this work or the perceived importance of competencies to those who would be affected by them.

When individuals received feedback from the development programme regarding their behaviour, they disputed the relevance of the development advice. The messages individuals were taking from pay and grading appeared to be more real and relevant than the messages from the training and development specialists.

Pay linked purely to competencies misses the contribution of actual work outputs achieved. For example, if an individual was good at planning, decision-making, teamwork and influencing, but didn't meet his or her sales targets, an organisation

---

Blinkered banking

Several years ago, an international bank began to develop a wholly competency-based pay scheme – on the misguided assumption that if people did things in the right way, they would do the right things in the right way. The scheme was trialled in the United States and after three years was finally abandoned.

Individuals in the organisation quickly realised that rewards were tied to development and not to activities or output. Some individuals focused as much time as possible on development and were rewarded for doing so – usually at the cost of output from the job. Consequently, development costs rocketed, output actually dropped, and the pay bill increased.

should surely be questioning what value that individual was bringing to the organisation. The same can be said for just paying on outputs. For example, if an individual exceeds his or her sales targets but does it by working long hours (because poor at planning) and upsetting everyone he or she meets on the way, then, again, an organisation using a competency framework should surely question whether it really does value the behaviours it has endorsed in the competency framework.

If an organisation states that competencies are important, surely this should link to the pay policy?

Making job value appear more open

Many job evaluation systems are complex, and in order to understand them and use them effectively, job analysts have to be trained in various techniques. This can often make job analysis a bit of a mystery to most people in the organisation. And, as with many mysteries, folklore builds up. Although it is jobs that are graded, it is people who hold them, and people understand that their pay will be affected by what grade their job is evaluated at. If individuals believe that budgets and the number of people they manage make all the difference between one grade and the next, there is a danger that, come job re-evaluation, there will be some considerable emphasis on those features of their jobs. This is perhaps more of an issue in today's flatter organisations where often one of the rare chances of 'promotion' is to get one's job re-graded!

The advantage of using a competency-based approach is that the competency framework is available for everyone to see. It can be made quite clear that the competencies in someone's role/job profile are the ones that were not only used to recruit them but also the ones which contributed to their job grade, and will form the framework for some of their performance objectives. Obviously, this still keeps other aspects of the job evaluation system 'hidden' but it is a step in the direction of openness.

Rewarding over-achievement

We mentioned in the grading section of this chapter that some organisations overlay their competency framework on their grading structure to help decide on levels of pay. Obviously, each job is likely to require a wide range of different competencies and the organisation has to decide which ones should directly link with pay.

If achievement of a certain level of competency is rewarded, then the question of over-achievement must be considered. Is the organisation willing to pay more for competency levels achieved over and above those required for a current job? There may be times when this is desirable – for example, when a pool of talent is being nurtured for succession-planning reasons or when a learning culture is being encouraged. However, even when it is desirable, the organisation should make it clear

- how people can over-achieve
- who is going to rate their performance
- what will happen if over-achievement equals levels of competency that are outside the pay limit for their grade.

There is a balance to be achieved when rewarding over-achievement of competency levels. This is between encouraging people to improve to meet whatever the objective of the policy is, and the danger of raising competency levels beyond that which is required in the short or medium term. There is also the issue of paying people for competencies, or competency levels, that they may never use. This may result in the salary bill's being larger than has been budgeted for.

Other issues for consideration with pay and grading

Overpayment

With competency-based pay schemes which increase basic pay as a result of the achievement of competency, the obvious – and indeed the desired – result is that high-achieving job-holders are paid more highly than the others in their grade.

Such a differential is the desired result. But what happens if the high-achiever does not use all of the competencies that he or she has obtained? Some organisations may find this a price that they are prepared to pay, but for others it may lead to an unacceptably high salary bill.

One way of rewarding the achievement of competency is to create the incentive without rewarding it with money. For example, if career progression relies on an individual's demonstrating a willingness to achieve levels of competency over and above those that are required for his or her current job, this would not only be an incentive but would also restrict this achievement to those for whom career development is a motivator.

If monetary reward is considered important, however, an organisation may wish to consider bonus payments. These can be one-off payments for the achievement of competency. They reward achievement without unnecessarily increasing the salary budget over the long term. However, issues such as why people would be motivated to achieve such levels of competency and what the long-term benefit is to the organisation have clearly to be considered before introducing such a scheme.

Team v individual pay

Many organisations are putting more and more emphasis on teams. Now that multi-functioning teams, matrix management and core and peripheral worker structures are becoming more *en vogue*, there is a realisation that organisational success is often better achieved through teamwork than through the efforts of a number of individuals loosely called a 'team' merely because they report to the same manager.

As this emphasis on teams becomes stronger, the issue of how to reward the people in those teams is featuring higher on the agenda of pay and reward specialists. How do you motivate and reward performance at an individual level while maintaining an emphasis on the team?

This issue becomes particularly relevant in organisations where a competency framework has been established which focuses on job competency requirements which are, on the whole, expected to be fulfilled by one individual.

It would appear that there is a third element being added in these circumstances. Not only is performance concerned with the individual's achievement of objectives in relation to outputs (the 'what') and inputs (the 'how', or competencies) but it centres on how the team performs as a whole in relation to team goals.

Pay, in these circumstances, could be broken down into these three elements, so that team members earn a bonus for their team-based contribution (ie that which is achievable only because individuals in that team work together) and individuals are rewarded for their personal contributions to the team.

If an organisation empowers team members to act collectively to manage resources and make decisions (within pre-agreed parameters), it is conceivable that team pay could be based on outputs and individual pay based on inputs. Measurement of performance would be against pre-agreed requirements for the organisation and the team. In a fully empowered team it could be argued that any shortfall of an individual in terms of his or her outputs would have to be addressed by the team because it could affect the overall team pay. Measurement of performance on an individual basis could then be based entirely on the behavioural indicators in the competency framework. We have not seen this type of approach taken in any organisation yet: we wait with interest to see how the issue is tackled.

Development v reward

One of the drawbacks to tying performance in so closely with pay is the distraction it causes when discussing less than acceptable performance. Knowing that any acknowledgement that a competency is not a strength may result in an erosion of the pay rise that could be coming their way may lead to people's playing down the issue or avoiding it altogether. It is also a distraction for the manager, who may not want to de-motivate a staff member in this way.

The issue can be tackled by setting learning objectives. This may be particularly relevant for trainees in the job who can't be expected to achieve the same level of output or competency as their more experienced peers. A learning objective will focus on the achievement of certain levels of competency or output within certain time-frames and with agreed support. Assuming that the trainee is already being paid at the lower end of the pay range, he or she can still achieve acceptable performance ratings while discussing development and progress. The setting of learning objectives is covered in the training and development chapter (Chapter 5).

Another way of tackling this issue is to split the discussion about achievement of objectives away from the discussion about development needs. If objectives are clearly established, measurement of performance against them should be relatively easy. The output from this discussion can then feed into pay. Another discussion, held at a completely different time and following a different cycle, can then be held on the subject of training and development needs.

As long as pay and performance are closely linked, this issue will never be completely resolved. However, there are ways to minimise the distraction of pay when discussing performance, and organisations should think through carefully how they are going to tackle the issue.

In brief

The close link between grading structures and the pay that is attached to the jobs that fall within that structure make these two issues difficult to separate. However, they are both to do with an attempt to apply relative values of a job or an individual to the organisation. The value of a job or role is indicated by its relative position in the hierarchy of the grading systems. The value of individuals is indicated by the job or role they are doing, how they are doing it, and the rewards they receive.

In this chapter we have focused on the links that some organisations make between pay and performance (PRP), such that the level of financial reward that an individual receives is directly linked to his or her performance in the job. There are many reasons why organisations introduce PRP and many factors that affect how the system is designed. Competency-based pay is where there is a direct link between competency ratings and pay. However, there is often a competency element in PRP, and organisations which measure competency in performance reviews will often link the ratings of both outputs and inputs to pay.

Very few organisations are using competencies alone to evaluate jobs and create grading structures. In most cases, the contribution that competencies make to these activities is in providing additional information to create a more rounded picture of a job than concentrating only on what outputs are produced. If competencies are used in other people-management activities, the message is that these behaviours are valued. If job evaluation is about measuring the elements of a job which an organisation values, it makes sense to include competencies in that process.

Once a grading system has been agreed, pay bands or pay positions are overlaid. Many factors influence what levels of pay are agreed. Pay is the financial reward which individuals receive for the work they do. Not all components of pay are necessarily tied to performance, even in PRP systems. For example, some bonuses may be paid regardless of grade or individual performance. However, the elements that are affected by performance tie in with competencies where these are measured.

The issue of performance measurement is covered in another chapter (Chapter 4). But how the outcome of that performance review links with pay is an area that needs careful thought and clear communication to all involved in the process. Concentration on payment just for results (outputs) misses the important aspect of *how* a job is performed. Payment just for the achievement of competency misses the important aspect of producing results.

Pay and grading are complex issues and there are no clear answers or 'right' way of tackling them. The key role that competencies can play in these processes is to improve the completeness of information being used to grade jobs and allocate pay. Competencies are therefore a factor in the process, not the process itself. Organisations that take an integrative approach to their competency framework need to ensure that the value they are placing on behaviours is endorsed through all of its people-management processes – including pay and grading.

7   CONCLUSION

Background

Behavioural criteria, similar to what we now know as competencies, have been around for a long time in various forms. Typically, these criteria were specific to one application. Organisations drew up criteria for recruitment and selection, training and development, pay and grading and performance review, but it was unusual for these to be linked, let alone actually be the same criteria. The competency movement promised one set of criteria for all applications – a generic framework which could be understood and used by all people involved in managing performance.

Far from being the latest management fad, competency frameworks introduced an element into all people-management applications which, in many cases, had been missing. This was the focus on *how* people do their jobs. Previously much attention had been paid to the outputs of a job and little paid to the behaviours of the people producing those outputs. It became apparent that behaviour mattered – particularly as demands for high-quality products and customer service were often forcing organisations to pay attention to the 'how' of people's job performance to ensure that they retained or won market advantage.

Competency frameworks are likely to be a passing fad only if organisations introduce them without considering some key issues:

❏ why a competency framework is needed
❏ how the framework will be used
❏ what competencies can do (and cannot do)
❏ what the users of the framework want from competencies.

In this book we have tried to address these issues by proposing that in order to use competencies effectively, organisations need to

❑ avoid confusion over their definition
❑ structure them in a way which makes them easy to use
❑ understand their role in applications
❑ produce them to expected quality standards.

The quality standards mentioned stated that competencies must

❑ be clear and easy to understand
❑ be relevant to all staff who will be affected by the framework
❑ take account of expected changes
❑ have discrete elements (eg behavioural indicators, competencies which do not overlap)
❑ be fair to all affected by its use.

Only when the purpose of a framework is clear and the quality standards understood is it advisable for organisations to think about introducing a framework.

Producing a competency framework

Whether an organisation uses a standard competency framework produced elsewhere or whether it uses one that has been adapted or designed for its own circumstances is a decision only it can make. 'Off-the-shelf' frameworks prevent jobholders in the organisation from being involved in the design process and can minimise buy-in when the framework is introduced. The organisation may also find that they are making compromises to fit in with the 'off-the-shelf' framework – especially in relation to their stated values or the culture of the organisation. Ideally, behaviours in the competency framework should endorse behaviours that are considered important. However, as mentioned above, the purpose and use of the framework has to be offset against other considerations such as the availability of resources (budget, time, etc).

Where organisations design their own competency frameworks, these need to be developed in a disciplined way using a planned structure, appropriate techniques and people with the necessary skills. In Chapter 2 we identified three key principles to help ensure that the framework meets the quality standards previously mentioned:

1   Involve the people who will be affected by the framework.
2   Keep people informed about what is happening and why.
3   Behaviours described in the competencies must be relevant to all those who will be affected by them as well as to organisational needs and intended applications.

We also listed a number of steps that can be taken to produce a competency framework to ensure that a structured, disciplined approach is taken. The key issues we identified that should be taken into account when designing a competency framework include:

❑   whether to produce a generic framework or a range of frameworks for use in different parts of the organisation
❑   whether to have levels within each competency to differentiate between groups of behaviours
❑   whether any levels introduced are incremental (ie whether all behaviours in the 'lower' levels may be assumed to be evident in the 'higher' levels).

One factor when considering these issues is what applications the competency framework will be used for and how its use will fit into the policies and processes for those applications. In this book we have considered four key applications in people management:

❑   selection
❑   reviewing performance
❑   training and development
❑   pay and grading.

The use of competencies in applications

Selection

In Chapter 3 we discussed how organisations could use competencies to help establish a match between people and the demands of work before placing them in a job or role. The best match is likely to be where individuals can show that they can produce the outputs that are required in the job in the way that the organisation requires. Competencies will support the selection process by providing a framework against which the 'how' part of the job can be measured. The use of competencies alone is not a guarantee of cast iron selection decisions, however, because there are factors other than behaviour that must be taken into account.

Reviewing performance

When discussing performance reviews in Chapter 4 we covered all occasions where the performance of an individual is measured – not just appraisal interviews. As with selection, the best performers are likely to be those who not only produce what the organisation requires of them but do so in a way which fits with organisational values and approach.

Competencies will support the process of reviewing performance by providing a framework against which the 'how' part of the job-holder's performance can be measured. We also pointed out, however, that performance is affected by a wide range of factors and that success in a job is not just a matter of going about things in the right way. In other words, to review and measure an individual's complete performance requires an understanding of more than just his or her behaviour.

Training and development

In Chapter 5 we explored the two key purposes of training and development – ie to ensure that the competencies of individuals in an organisation are sufficient to meet both current and future needs of the organisation and of the individual. We identified the ways in which competency frameworks can assist in all key stages of training and development, from identifying the original need to designing the event and measuring not only the success of the event but the progress of individuals through structured programmes. The focus of training and development can be either at competency level or at the level of component parts that contribute to that competency (which would include the training of specific techniques). We also put forward the view that using competencies in training and development processes is not enough to ensure that learning takes place. It depends on many other factors.

Pay and grading

When considering pay and grading in Chapter 6 we looked at both issues together. We also focused on pay directly affected by an individual's performance. Job evaluation systems and grading systems are often produced using techniques and processes created before competencies were developed. Of all the applications we have covered in this book, job evaluation and grading systems are the ones in which competencies are least likely to be used. Pay is often set within pay bands or at specific points on a scale against benchmarks which don't include the explicit consideration of competencies. It is in the decisions made about the actual pay an individual receives that competency frameworks seem to be most effectively used. However, focusing only on the achievement of levels of competency may lead to a pay budget which is not justified when compared to the outputs of the individuals in the organisation. When considering pay and grading, therefore, factors other than competencies have to be taken into account.

The contribution of competencies

In this book we have shown that a well-structured competency framework can contribute to each of the applications we have discussed. In some way this goes toward fulfilling the promise of competencies, in that we have shown how one framework can extend to each application.

We have also shown how these applications can be enhanced through the use of competencies in key stages of the process. Competency frameworks can assist in

❑ information-gathering
❑ evaluation and assessment
❑ decision-making.

A competency framework can provide a set of criteria to gather information and can also assist in the design of information-gathering tools and exercises. Competencies can provide benchmarks for comparing actual performance with desired performance. They can also inform decision rules, such as those established for performance ratings and pay awards.

A key theme that has run throughout the whole book is that although all of the people-management applications discussed make use of competencies in the above ways, they provide only a limited focus. That is, competencies focus only on behavioural performance. While behaviour is clearly an important issue, other information that is essential for these applications include:

❏ what a person does and achieves (outputs)
❏ the context in which he or she operates
❏ personal factors that influence performance
❏ organisational factors that influence performance.

Even with all this information there are no guarantees of success because these applications also require:

❏ appropriate processes
❏ relevant and valid tools
❏ skilled practitioners.

These points apply particularly where a generic competency framework is introduced. This type of framework is, by its nature, very general, involving broad statements of behaviour. To make it usable it has to be accompanied by procedures and tools for adapting it to meet the needs of a particular area or application in the organisation.

Some organisations have elevated competencies to be the prime focus within some applications. This results in an unbalanced approach and can detract from, or even displace, the actual purpose of the application.

It is essential that organisations invest time and effort in designing a complete process – one that involves all of the factors mentioned above. Competency frameworks should not shift the focus from other factors of good practice: they should enhance them. It is the application and the purpose of the application that is important and should be the primary focus of activity. The application will be compromised if any one factor is elevated to primary status, including competencies.

Where do we go from here?

One of the topics not covered in this book is that of technical competence. It would be untrue to argue that it was left out because technical competence cannot be written in behavioural terms. In many organisations technical competencies contain statements of required knowledge and specific technical skills. However, in other organisations technical competencies contain statements of required technical and/or academic qualifications. The latter form of competencies are frequently found in technical specialist organisations such as in chemistry and engineering.

Technical competencies which contain statements of qualifications can be difficult to generalise and apply in organisations, and can contribute to a hierarchy that is largely qualification-based. However, in many situations it is more helpful to know how an individual would use his or her technical knowledge and expertise. In these situations it should be possible to describe technical competency in terms of what one would observe a competent person doing with his or her knowledge and expertise. For example, one behavioural indicator might read 'Applies knowledge in specialist areas to generate models which describe how systems interact.'

Technology-based organisations trying to break free of a technocratic hierarchy may well find it worth investing in development of behavioural-based technical competencies. To our knowledge, very few organisations have attempted to define technical competency in behavioural terms. However, for completeness we suspect that this form of competency is likely to become more common in the future.

As we have highlighted in this book, competencies can make a significant contribution to all key people-management processes. Because we see the continuing focus on people as key assets within an organisation, competencies are here to stay – in one form or other. A well-designed competency framework does provide the common language for any situation or process in which the behaviour of the people in the organisation is key. It is therefore likely that competencies will feature more and more in the discussion of such issues as:

❏ culture change
❏ values
❏ organisational strategy
❏ quality standards
❏ equal opportunities.

Techniques for developing competencies may evolve but it is unlikely that radical new techniques will be developed – not least because it is time to move on to look at other aspects of performance. It is more important that organisations develop and employ processes to ensure that competencies are embedded into appropriate applications and that they are working for the business. In addition, attention should be given to ensuring that the applications themselves are well-designed and well-implemented.

With well-designed and well-implemented processes using well-designed and valid competencies, the next challenge will be to develop a better understanding and improved techniques for defining and using the other factors that affect performance. This is an area in which major changes and very significant gains are possible – we already know that our current best attempts to predict performance, though useful, present only a small fraction of the actual picture.

Appropriate research could provide a much better understanding of how the various factors interact to enhance or restrict performance, and much greater control over performance management and predicting performance will be possible. However, as indicated throughout this book, there are many factors that influence performance, and managing the necessary information could therefore become complex. Computer-based systems, which can learn from examples of effective performance management, may provide users with the necessary ability to manage the variety and volume of data likely to be involved.

Competencies can continue to make significant contributions to people-management practices and processes. These contributions rely on good design and skilful use. Whereas a wider view of factors that influence context and output is essential to ensure that the application fulfils its purpose, ignoring behavioural performance will flaw these applications.

The early promise of competencies as a common set of criteria has, to some degree, been achieved. It is now time to put competencies back into perspective – alongside the other factors critical for managing performance.

APPENDIX 1:
SAMPLE COMPETENCY FRAMEWORK

WORKING WITH PEOPLE: Managing relationships	**Level 1: Builds relationships internally** Adapts personal style to develop relationships with colleagues. Adapts form and presentation of information to meet needs of the audience. Identifies and maintains regular contact with individuals who depend on or who influence own work.
	Level 2: Builds relationships externally Takes account of the impact of own role on the needs of external contacts. Maintains regular two-way communication with external contacts. Identifies and nurtures external contacts who can contribute to the business.
	Level 3: Maintains external networks Takes account of different cultural styles and values when dealing with external organisations. Actively manages external contacts as a business network. Identifies and makes use of events for developing external network.

WORKING WITH PEOPLE: Teamworking	**Level 1: Is a team member** Encourages colleagues to contribute in teams. Listens and gives credit to contributions which others make in teams. Shares learning and information with colleagues.
	Level 2: Supports team members Encourages all team members to make useful contributions. Identifies when team members need support, and provides it. Responds positively to the contributions of other team members.
	Level 3: Provides direction for the team Uses knowledge of individuals' strengths, interests and development needs to delegate tasks. Provides regular feedback to the team. Ensures that team members understand their individual and collective responsibilities.
WORKING WITH PEOPLE: Influencing	**Level 1: Projects a positive image** Presents oral and written communication succinctly and with regard to its impact on the recipient. Presents self in a manner appropriate to the situation. Refers positively to the organisation, its people and its services.
	Level 2: Influences the thinking of others Presents relevant and well-reasoned arguments. Presents own points of view with conviction. Adapts and develops arguments to achieve results desired.

	Level 3: Changes the opinions of others Approaches negotiations with the objective of achieving a win-win outcome. Ensures that people likely to be affected by any new activity have been involved in developing the activity. Elicits views of others and uses them to develop counter-arguments or new positions.
WORKING WITH INFORMATION: Gathering and analysing information	**Level 1: Gathers and maintains information** Identifies and uses appropriate sources of information. Accurately identifies the type and form of information required. Obtains relevant information and maintains it in appropriate formats. **Level 2: Checks and analyses information** Establishes accuracy and relevance of information. Extracts key patterns and trends from information. Identifies links between different sets of information. Simplifies information for interpretation and presentation. **Level 3: Uses information to analyse the business** Uses a range of information to evaluate business performance. Identifies new opportunities for the business. Makes predictions for business performance from trends in business and market information.

WORKING WITH INFORMATION: Decision-making	**Level 1: Day-to-day decisions** Follows pre-set procedures where required. Obtains and uses necessary information to make decisions. Regularly reviews and agrees scope of decision-making for their role. Refers decision to others when appropriate.
	Level 2: Ensures that decisions are made Seeks buy-in for decisions where appropriate. Makes unpopular decisions when required. Takes responsibility for making decisions where necessary to move things forward.
	Level 3: High-level decision-making Decisions contain acceptable levels of risk. Decisions made with limited information when appropriate. Argues for support for decisions at all levels.
DEVELOPING THE BUSINESS: Personal development	**Level 1: Develops self** Builds own knowledge of the organisation, its people and its services. Seeks opportunities to develop own skills. Accepts feedback constructively. Regularly reviews and updates personal development plans.
	Level 2: Develops others Agrees and implements 'SMART' development action plans. Seeks and gives constructive feedback. Provides support for individuals when putting learning into practice. Regularly reviews progress on development.

	Level 3: Develops a culture for learning Ensures that development plans and activities contribute to business needs. Ensures that processes and procedures encourage learning. Ensures that resources are available to support learning at all levels in the organisation.
DEVELOPING THE BUSINESS: Generating and building on ideas	**Level 1: Participates in the generation of ideas** Actively participates in events for generating ideas. Positively questions established ways of doing things. Actively listens to and considers ideas presented by others.
	Level 2: Develops ideas into solutions Develops new processes or practices to accommodate new ideas. Assesses feasibility of ideas for the business. Promotes leading ideas with energy and enthusiasm.
	Level 3: Encourages an environment for developing ideas Provides opportunities and resources for people to share ideas. Provides constructive feedback on how ideas are being progressed. Provides support for all individuals to offer constructive criticism of new or established ideas.

ACHIEVING RESULTS: Planning	**Level 1: Prioritises day-to-day workload** Develops daily work plans from job objectives. Accurately prioritises key tasks. Avoids negative impact of own actions on others.
	Level 2: Plans to meet departmental objectives Accurately estimates resources to achieve plans. Builds alternative actions into plans to deal with likely contingencies. Communicates plans to relevant people.
	Level 3: Converts organisational plans into departmental plan Identifies contribution department can make to organisational objectives. Identifies activities and resources required to meet new objectives. Integrates departmental plan with activities of other departments.
	Level 4: Develops organisational plans Contributes to the development of a vision for the organisation. Identifies strategic activities to achieve the vision. Continually reviews and updates strategies as necessary.
ACHIEVING RESULTS: Deadline management	**Level 1: Takes responsibility for tasks** Takes responsibility to ensure commitments are met. Regularly reviews progress of tasks. Keeps people informed of progress on key tasks. Evaluates completed tasks.

	Level 2: Manages resources effectively Briefs others of expectations and their responsibilities. Informs other departments of commitments. Agrees changes to plans.
ACHIEVING RESULTS: Objective-setting	**Level 1: Contributes to setting of individual objectives** Ensures that objectives are achievable within already agreed commitments. Agrees appropriate success and measurement criteria. Identifies and highlights potential obstacles in achieving objectives.
	Level 2: Sets responsibilities Identifies and sets clear objectives. Establishes success and measurement criteria. Enrols the support of others for achieving objectives. Reviews and adapts objectives to meet changing needs.
	Level 3: Ensures that objectives contribute to organisational goals. Uses organisational goals to evaluate and prioritise objectives. Continually evaluates appropriateness of objectives at all levels. Delegates objectives appropriately.

APPENDIX 2: AN EXAMPLE OF PAIRED COMPARISONS

When comparing competencies for relative importance for a job, each competency is compared with every other competency for each key activity. In this example the comparisons have been made for just one key activity (KA1).

First a grid is produced which contains all of the competencies on each axis – for example:

KA1	C1	C2	C3	C4	C5	C6
C1						
C2						
C3						
C4						
C5						
C6						
Score						

Diagonal squares are shaded because a competency cannot be compared with itself. Next the comparisons begin. First competency one (C1) is compared with competency two (C2) by asking the question, 'For success in this key activity, is it more important that the job-holder has competency one or competency two?' If C1 is more important, it gets a score of 2; if it is equally important it gets a score of 1; and if it is less important, it gets a score of zero. It is essential that each time the question is asked, the competency in the top axis is the first to be referred to in the question and that the comparison is made with competencies in the side axis – ie the second competency referred to in the question must come from the side axis – otherwise, great confusion will reign. The score is placed in the appropriate cell below the first-mentioned competency. So, for instance, if C1 is more important than C2 for this key activity, a score of 2 would be placed in the grid thus:

KA1	C1	C2	C3	C4	C5	C6
C1						
C2	2					

The comparisons continue until the grid is full of scores, and then the scores in each column are added to produce competency scores:

KA1	C1	C2	C3	C4	C5	C6
C1		0	1	1	1	0
C2	2		0	1	0	1
C3	1	2		0	0	1
C4	1	1	2		1	0
C5	1	2	2	1		2
C6	2	1	1	2	0	
Score	7	6	6	5	2	4

In this example, C5 appears to be the least important competency for KA1. When grids have been completed for all key activities, an overall score can be produced for each competency. It is important to remember that the scores indicate perceived relative importance. A low score does not therefore necessarily mean that the competency is not important – or indeed that it is not essential.

This example is presented as an illustration only and is not intended to replace further reading or training.

Index